Near Dea Body Experiences

(Auspicious Births and Deaths)
Of the Prophets, Saints, Mystics and Sages in World Religions

Compiled By Marilynn Hughes

The Out-of-Body Travel Foundation!
www.outofbodytravel.org

For information, write to:

The Out-of-Body Travel Foundation!

www.outofbodytravel.org

MarilynnHughes@aol.com

If this book is unavailable from your local bookseller, it may be obtained directly from the Out-of-Body Travel Foundation by going to www.outofbodytravel.org.

Having worked primarily in radio broadcasting, Marilynn Hughes spent several years as a news reporter, producer and anchor before deciding to stay at home with her three children. She's experienced, researched, written, and taught about out-of-body travel since 1987.

Books by Marilynn Hughes:
Come to Wisdom's Door
How to Have an Out-of-Body Experience!

The Mysteries *of the* Redemption
A Treatise on **Out-of-Body Travel** and **Mysticism**

The Mysteries *of the* Redemption Series in Five Volumes
(Same Book - Choose Your Format!)
Prelude to a Dream
Passage to the Ancient
Medicine Woman Within a Dream
Absolute Dissolution of Body and Mind
The Mystical Jesus

GALACTICA
A Treatise on **Death, Dying and the Afterlife**

THE PALACE OF ANCIENT KNOWLEDGE
A Treatise on **Ancient Mysteries**

Near Death and Out-of-Body Experiences
(Auspicious Births and Deaths)
Of the Prophets, Saints, Mystics and Sages in World Religions

The Former Angel! - *A Children's Tale*

Dedication:
To the Prophets, Saints, Mystics and Sages from every Religion and Throughout time … That They Might Have Voice!

CONTENTS

Near Death and Out-of-Body Experiences

(Auspicious Births and Deaths)

Of the Prophets, Saints, Mystics and Sages in World Religions

Go to our Website at:

www.outofbodytravel.org

For more information!

INTRODUCTION

Near Death and Out-of-Body Experiences

(Auspicious Births and Deaths)

Of the Prophets, Saints, Mystics and Sages in World Religions

It is said in the ancient sacred texts of almost every world religion that the great prophets and saints often appear with 'auspicious signs.' Auspicious signs are special mystical circumstances and wonders around the birth, life and death of holy persons.

In order to fully understand the unity and diversity of the many faiths practiced in our world, we must know and understand these great moments in religious history. In examining the lives, experiences, teachings, (births and deaths), we find the mystic thread of unity which unites them all as one.

But what may also strike you is that although Out-of-Body Travel or Experiences are often considered as being outside the realm of religion - perhaps as something paranormal; you'll discover in these pages is that Out-of-Body Experiences are an integral part of the formation and continuation of every major and minor world religion although such experiences may be called by different names. If you take the time to search the ancient sacred texts, Out-of-Body Travel is actually quite common among most seekers throughout time and of every faith and creed.

How odd it is that it is now sometimes considered outside of the mainstream when in actuality, it is through Out-of-Body Experiences that most of our spiritual traditions have sprung and continued to maintain vitality.

And in knowing these events and happenings throughout religious history, we can more fully comprehend the royal family of God and how in apparent contradictory roles and missions, they come together to serve the One True God . . .

"Howsoever He so willeth, Howsoever He so pleaseth."
(Words of Baha'u'llah, Baha'i)

CHAPTER ONE
HINDUISM

Krishna
*("The Path of Yoga," By A.C. Bhaktivedanta Swami Prabhupada,
Bhaktivedanta Book Trust, 1995)*

Devaki (Mother of Krishna)
*("KRSNA," By A.C. Bhaktivedanta Swami Prabhupada,
Bhaktivedanta Book Trust, 1970)*

Auspicious Birth of the Prophet Krishna

The date of birth of the Prophet Krishna is not known, but it is known that Hinduism began about 3,000 B.C.E. Krishna was born to a royal family in great turmoil, and according to accounts of his life, he received his calling in early childhood.

"King Kamsa, the most powerful and tyrannical monarch of his time, had a sister whom he loved very tenderly. This beloved sister, Devaki, was about to marry Vasudeva. As a token of his fraternal affection the king presented the newly affianced couple with many costly gifts, and then declared that after their wedding he himself would drive their carriage."

"In due time he fulfilled this promise, and Devaki and Vasudeva were very happy at the thought of their singular good fortune in having as their driver the dreaded monarch of the surrounding territories. There were ovations and rejoicings as they drove along, and everywhere the people were filled with happiness."

"All went well until, of a sudden, King Kamsa heard a voice from the void saying: 'O thou foolish one, whom art thou driving so merrily? Knowest thou not that the eighth issue of her womb shall be the cause of thy death?'"

"At this the terrible Kamsa sprang from his seat. Drawing his sword he would have killed his sister then and there, had not Vasudeva interposed and prayed the king to spare the life of his newly married wife, reminding him that not Devaki but her eighth child would be the cause of his death, and promising, because of the king's fear, that each and every one of her children should be given over to Kamsa to deal with as he wished. Thus was King Kamsa pacified."

"When in the course of time children were born to Vasudeva and Devaki, the parents fulfilled their promise to Kamsa, who, one after another, killed seven of their children as soon as they were born. This of course caused much grief to Vasudeva and Devaki, but there was no way to escape from the hands of the tyrannical king."

"When at last the time for the birth of the eighth child was approaching, Kamsa ordered Vasudeva and Devaki to be cast into prison. Accordingly, both of them were thrown into the same dungeon and bound with the same chain."

"Being friendless and helpless, they were sorely troubled in their hearts. Their only consolation was in prayer to the almighty, all-loving God; and so they both prayed earnestly from the depths of their hearts, imploring him to protect them and their child. While thus ardently praying, they fell into a swoon. In the gloom of that unconsciousness a light suddenly flashed; and in that light the thick, dark cloud of misery vanished, and with it the accumulated sorrows of recent years. The sun of gladness and peace, the Lord of Love, appeared before them, healing the wounds in their hearts and cheering and exhilarating them with his benign smile. They were enveloped completely in his love; and presently they were more blissful still, for they heard him speak these sweet words: 'Father and mother, weep no more. I have come at last to your rescue and to the escape of all the good. Earth shall complain no longer. The days of the wicked are numbered. The wretched Kamsa shall die. Once again there will be peace and goodness on earth.'"

"'Open your eyes and see me born as your child. Carry me, father, to the house of thy good friend King Nanda in Gokula. His wife, the Queen Yasoda, has just now given birth to a daughter. Exchange me for that daughter. Bring her with thee to this dungeon, leaving me on the lap of Yasoda, who will be sleeping at the time. Nothing shall bar my path.'"

"So it came to pass that Krishna, who was to remove the bondage of humanity, was born in a prison cell belonging to the monarch Kamsa."

"Devaki kissed the sweet face of her child, forgetting all danger, but Vasudeva remembered the instructions received in vision. He clasped the child to his bosom, and at the moment he was ready to leave the prison his chains were loosened and the gates of the prison cell were opened wide. He crossed the river Yamuna, and, encountering not the least opposition, he exchanged his son for the infant daughter of Yasoda. Returning with the baby girl, he placed her on the lap of Devaki. The gates of the prison then closed, and he found himself once more in chains."

"Early in the morning Kamsa heard of the birth of a female child, and at once came to the prison to see the baby. Vasudeva implored him to spare the life of the child because there could be no cause of danger in a girl. But Kamsa paid no heed to his request. He caught the feet of the tiny baby firmly in his hands, lifted it high in the air, and was about to dash it against a stone, when behold, the infant slipped from his fierce, demoniac grip and assuming high above him the beautiful form of the Divine Mother, looked down upon him, and said: 'Wretch, dost thou think to avert the will of the almighty? Lo, thy destroyer is flourishing in Gokula.' After these words she vanished, and King Kamsa trembled."

The Srimad Bhagavatam, Book Tenth, Part I,
Translated by Swami Prabhavananda, Capricorn
Books, (Hinduism)

"Vasudeva saw that wonderful child born as a baby with four hands, holding conchshell, club, disc and lotus flower, decorated with the mark of Srivatsa, wearing the jeweled necklace of kaustubha stone, dressed in yellow silk, appearing dazzling like a bright blackish cloud, wearing a helmet bedecked with the vaidurya stone, valuable bracelets, earrings and similar other ornaments all over His body, and beautified by an abundance of hair on His head. Due to the extraordinary features of the child, Vasudeva was struck with wonder. How could a newly born child be so decorated? He could therefore understand that Lord Krsna had now appeared."

KRSNA, Volume 1, Chapter Three, Page 46, A.C.
Bhaktivedanta Swami Prabhupada, Bhaktivedanta
Book Trust, 1970 (Hinduism)

12

Auspicious Experience of the Prophet Krishna

"Arjuna: Out of compassion you have taught me the supreme mystery of the Self. Through your words my delusion is gone. You have explained the origin and end of every creature, O lotus-eyed one, and told me of your own supreme, limitless existence. Just as you have described your infinite glory, O Lord, now I long to see it. I want to see you as the supreme ruler of creation. O Lord, master of yoga, if you think me strong enough to behold it, show me your immortal Self. Sri Krishna: Behold, Arjuna, A million divine forms, with an infinite variety of color and shape. Behold the gods of the natural world, and many more wonders never revealed before. Behold the entire cosmos turning within my body, and the other things you desire to see. But these things cannot be seen with your physical eyes; therefore I give you spiritual vision to perceive my majestic power. Sanjaya: Having spoken these words, Krishna, the master of yoga, revealed to Arjuna his most exalted, lordly form. He appeared with an infinite number of faces, ornamented by heavenly jewels, displaying unending miracles and the countless weapons of his power. Clothed in celestial garments and covered with garlands, sweet-smelling with heavenly fragrances, he showed himself as the infinite Lord, the source of all wonders, whose face is everywhere. If a thousand suns were to rise in the heavens at the same time, the blaze of their light would resemble the splendor of that supreme spirit. There, within the body of the God of gods, Arjuna saw all the manifold forms of the universe united as one. Filled with amazement, his hair standing on end in ecstasy, he bowed before the Lord with joined palms."

The Bhagavad Gita, Chapter 11:1-14, Translated by Eknath Easwaran, Nilgiri Press, (Hinduism, Words of Krishna)

Auspicious Death of the Prophet Krishna

Krishna was considered to be an incarnation of God, a transcendental man-god who was not entirely a physical being during his lifetime. Therefore, there are no accounts of his death in the scriptures of Hinduism, but only his continual transcendence of all worlds.

"The gigantic form of Maha-Visnu, greatly pleased, smiled pleasingly and spoke as follows.' My dear Krsna and Arjuna, I was very eager to see you both . . . I have been expecting to see you both at this palace. You have appeared in the material world as My incarnations in order to minimize the force of the demoniac persons who burden the world . . . Although you are both complete in yourselves, to protect the devotees and to annihilate the demons, and especially to establish religious principles in the world so that peace and tranquility may continue, you are teaching the basic principles of factual religion so that the people of the world may follow you and thereby be peaceful . . . '"

"Arjuna, however, was struck with great

wonder after visiting the transcendental world by the grace of Lord Krsna. And by the grace of Krsna he could understand that whatever opulence there may be within this material world is an emanation from Him. Any opulent position a person may have within this material world is due to Krsna's mercy. One should therefore always be . . . in complete gratefulness to Lord Krsna, because whatever one may possess is all bestowed by Him."

KRSNA, Volume 2, Chapter 89, Page 455, A.C. Bhaktivedanta Swami Prabhupada, Bhaktivedanta Book Trust, 1970 (Hinduism)

"When Uddhava was thus taught the path of yoga, and had listened to the very words of the glorious Sri Krishna, his eyes filled with tears of gratitude . . . Uddhava: 'Thy very presence, O Lord of the universe, has removed delusion from my heart. Can the chill of darkness and fear overcome him who stands by a fire? Thou hast of thy grace restored to me, thy servant, the lamp of knowledge. How can he who knows thy grace forsake thee and seek another? Obeisance unto thee, O great Yogin! And be thou pleased to tell me, who have taken refuge in thee, how I may grow in devotion to thy Lotus Feet.'"

"Sri Krishna: 'Go, Uddhava, at my command, to my hermitage called Badarika, where at the very sight of the Alakananda, the sacred river that sprang from my Feet, all thy sins, O beloved Friend, will be washed away, and by bathing in its waters, or by merely touching them, thou shalt be purified. There, clad in bark, living on wild roots and fruits, averse to pleasures, patient under all hardships, calm and poised, with thy senses under control and thy mind concentrated, possessed of knowledge and realization, reflecting on what I have told thee and thou hast well learned, with thy speech and mind directed towards me, follow my path. Thus shalt thou transcend the limitations of the three gunas and attain to me, the supreme."

The Srimad Bhagavatam, Book Eleventh, Part XXI, Translated by Swami Prabhavananda, Capricorn Books, (Hinduism)

"One who has not merely studied the Scriptures but has realized in himself the experience recorded in them, and has known the truth of the Self, sees the universe as illusory. He surrenders his knowledge, as well as the way to knowledge, unto me."

"For I am the goal of the wise man, and I am the way. I am his prosperity. I am his heaven. There is nothing dearer to him than I."

The Srimad Bhagavatam, Book Eleventh, Part XII, Translated by Swami Prabhavananda, Capricorn Books, (Hinduism)

"I have learned what is to be known. With thy blessing I will now control my senses, and concentrate my mind, with all its desires and ambitions, on the Lotus Feet of Sri Krishna, my chosen Avatara, the door which leads to the vision of God and to union with Brahman, the all-pervading existence."

The Srimad Bhagavatam, Book Twelfth, Part I,

Translated by Swami Prabhavananda, Capricorn Books, (Hinduism)

"For him the universe is his garment and the Lord not separate from himself."
The Upanishads, Paramahamsa Upanishad, No. 4, Translated by Eknath Easwaran, Nilgiri Press, (Hinduism)

Death According to the Prophet Krishna

"Those who remember me at the time of death will come to me. Do not doubt this. Whatever occupies the mind at the time of death determines the destination of the dying; always they will tend toward that state of being. Therefore, remember me at all times and fight on. With your heart and mind intent on me, you will surely come to me. When you make your mind one-pointed through regular practice of meditation, you will find the supreme glory of the Lord . . . Remembering me at the time of death, close down the doors of the senses and place the mind in the heart. Then, while absorbed in meditation, focus all energy upwards to the head. Repeating in this state the divine Name, the syllable Om that represents the changeless Brahman, you will go forth from the body and attain the supreme goal."
The Bhagavad Gita, Chapter 8: 5-8, 12-13, Translated by Eknath Easwaran, Nilgiri Press, (Hinduism, Words of Krishna)

"At the moment of death the sum of all the experiences of life on earth comes to the surface of the mind - for in the mind are stored all impressions of past deeds - and the dying man then becomes absorbed in these experiences. Then comes complete loss of memory. Next there arises before man's mind the vision of his life to come, a vision regulated by his impressions of his past deeds; and he no longer recollects his life on earth. This complete forgetfulness of his past identity is death."

"His complete acceptance of another state and identification with a new body is said to be his birth. He no longer remembers his past life, and, though he has existed before, he considers himself newly born."

"Like the flame of a lamp or the current of a river, the bodies of creatures, with the imperceptible passing of time, are in constant motion. Hence they are in a sense continually born and continually dying. Is the flame of the lamp one and the same now as before? Is the current of water one and the same always? Is man, if identified with the body, the same man today that he was yesterday?"

"Verily is there neither birth nor death to the real man: he is immortal. All else is delusion."

"Conception, embryonic state, birth, childhood, boyhood, youth, middle age, and death - these are different states of the body and affect not the real man. But man, because of his attachment to the gunas, identifies himself ignorantly with these desirable or undesirable states, which belong of a surety to the body and not to the Self. A few, however, who are wise, who have attained knowledge, give up this identification and find eternal life."

The Srimad Bhagavatam, Book Eleventh, Part XV, Page 286-287, Translated by Swami Prabhavananda, Capricorn Books, (Hinduism)

Auspicious Experience of the Prophet Nanak

Nanak Founder of the Sikh's
("Religions of the World" By Lewis M. Hopfe, Section on Sikhism,
Prentice Hall, 1994)

"When Nanak was 30 years old, he received what he took to be a divine call. One day he failed to return from his morning bath in the river. His friends, finding his clothes on the riverbank, dragged the waters in a vain attempt to find his body. Three days later Nanak reappeared. At first he gave no explanation for his absence but made only the following cryptic statement: 'There is neither Hindu nor Mussulman [Muslim], so whose path shall I choose? I shall follow God's path. God is neither Hindu nor Mussulman and the path which I follow is God's.' Later Nanak told them that in a vision he had been carried up to God's presence. God gave Nanak a cup of nectar and then the following message: 'I am with thee. I have given thee happiness, and I shall make happy all who take thy name. Go thou and repeat my Name; cause others to repeat it. Abide unspoiled by the world. Practice charity, perform ablutions, worship and meditate. My name is God, the primal Brahma. Thou art the Holy Guru.'"

Religions of the World, Third Edition, Sikhism, Nanak's Career, Multiple Authors, St. Martin's Press, 1993, (Compilation)

Auspicious Experience of Ramakrishna

Sri Ramakrishna
("The Gospel of Sri Ramakrishna," By M., Ramakrishna Vivekananda Center, 1942)

"The Vedas speak of seven planes where the mind dwells. When the mind is immersed in worldliness it dwells in the three lower planes - at the navel, the organ of generation, and the organ of evacuation. In that state the mind loses all its higher visions - it broods only on 'woman and gold.' The fourth plane of the mind is at the heart. When the mind dwells there, one has the first glimpse of spiritual consciousness. One sees light all around. Such a man, perceiving the divine light, becomes speechless with wonder and says: 'Ah! What is this? What is this?' His mind does not go downward to the objects of the world."

"The fifth plane of the mind is at the throat. When the mind reaches this, the aspirant becomes free from all ignorance and illusion. He does not enjoy talking or hearing about anything but God. If people talk about worldly things, he leaves the place at once."

"The sixth plane is at the forehead. When the mind reaches it, the aspirant sees the form of God day and night. But even then a little trace of ego remains. At the sight of that incomparable beauty of God's form, one becomes intoxicated and rushes forth to touch and embrace it. But one doesn't succeed. It is like the light inside a lantern. One feels as if one could touch the light, but one cannot on account of the pane of glass."

"In the top of the head is the seventh plane. When the mind rises there, one goes into samadhi. Then the Brahmajnani directly perceives Brahman. But in that state his body does not last many days. He remains unconscious of the outer world."

The Gospel of Sri Ramakrishna, Chapter 6, Page 150-151, By M, Ramakrishna-Vivekananda Center, 1942, (Hinduism)

Auspicious Experience of Sri Sarada Devi

Sri Sarada Devi (Wife of Sri Ramakrishna)
("The Gospel of Sri Ramakrishna," By M., Ramakrishna Vivekananda Center, 1942)

"When the Master departed from this life, I felt like going away too. He appeared before me and said, 'No, you must remain. There is so much yet to be done.' In the end I too understood how much there was to be done. He used to say, 'The people of Calcutta are squirming like worms in the dark. Take care of them.'"

The Teachings of Sri Sarada Devi, Chapter XII, No. 1, Sri Ramakrishna Math, (Hinduism)

Auspicious Experience of Paramahamsa Yogananda

Paramahansa Yogananda
("Man's Eternal Quest," By Paramahansa Yogananda, Self-Realization Fellowship, 1975)

"This vision I had during an ecstatic state of God-realization. I saw myself sitting on a little patch of the Milky Way, beholding the vast universe around me. As God became manifest, all things that had before seemed inanimate were consciously celebrating His homecoming within my consciousness - in the mansion of light."

"Thy mansion of the heavens is lit by perennial auroral displays of mystic lights. Stellar systems arch across the trackless highways of eternity that lead to Thy secret home. Comet-peacocks spread their plumes of rays and dance in wild delight in Thy garden of many moons. The planetary dance glides in stately rhythm, awaiting Thy homecoming. "

"I sit on a little patch of the Milky Way and behold the glory of Thy kingdom spread round me - endlessly, everywhere. The festivities of the heavens are dazzling with fireworks of shooting stars - hurled across the blue vaults by unseen bands of Thine obedient, devoted forces. Meteorites skip, glow, swoon, and fall to earth - mad with Thy joy."

" . . . Heavenly lights have opened their gates. Bonfires of nebulous mists are heralding Thine approach. The steady sentinels of sun and moon are patiently waiting for Thy homecoming. And I - I am running wild, dancing in my little body on my little earth, or skimming over the Milky Way, coaxing everything, every atom, every speck of consciousness, to open its gates and let Thy light shine through completely, driving darkness forevermore from Thy cosmic kingdom, which without Thee was a lonesome wilderness of matter."

Songs of the Soul, Thy Homecoming, Page 108-109, Self-Realization Fellowship, 1983, (Hinduism)

Auspicious Words of Maharishi Mahesh Yogi

Maharishi Mahesh Yogi
*("The Science of Being and Art of Living," By Maharishi Mahesh Yogi,
International SRM Publications, 1963)*

"Freedom from karma is gained by attaining the status of eternal Being. By the action of allowing the mind to reach Being it is possible to create a situation without ourselves whereby we shall always produce good influences for ourselves and for the entire universe. At the same time we rise above the binding influence of action and live a life of eternal freedom."

"This is the philosophy of karma. It not only deals with right and wrong and the far reaching influences of action, but also suggests a technique to rise above its binding influence."

The Science of Being and Art of Living, Chapter Two, Karma and the Art of Being, Page 142, Maharishi Mahesh Yogi, International SRM Publications, 1966, (Hinduism: Transcendental Meditation)

Auspicious Words of A.C. Bhaktivedanta Swami Prabhupada

A.C. Bhaktivedanta Swami Prabhupada
*("The Path of Yoga," By A.C. Bhaktivedanta Swami Prabhupada,
Bhaktivedanta Book Trust, 1995)*

"'The single one almighty God is supplying all necessities to millions and trillions of living entities. Therefore, we should not demand anything of God, because our demands are already met. The supplies are already there. We should simply try to love God."
The Path of Yoga, Chapter Eight, Page 100-101, A.C. Bhaktivedanta Swami Prabhupada, The Bhaktivedanta Book Trust, 1995, (Hinduism: Hare Krishna)

CHAPTER TWO
JUDAISM

'Moses'
*("The Law and the Prophets," Carlo Dolci - Artist, Pitti Palace,
Florence, Page 166, Harry N. Abrams, Inc.)*

Auspicious Birth of the Prophet Moses

The Prophet Moses is said to have lived
sometime around 1500 B.C.E., born in Egypt to a
Hebrew family but raised in opulence as the son of
Pharaoh's daughter. Receiving his call later in life, an
exact age is not known for the commencement of
Moses' mission, although we do know it occurred
after a lengthy exile and after he took a wife and had
children.

"Then Pharaoh charged all his people, saying,
'Every boy that is born you shall throw into the Nile,

but let every girl live.' A certain man of the house of Levi went and married a Levite woman. The woman conceived and bore a son; and when she saw how beautiful he was, she hid him for three months. When she could hide him no longer, she got a wicker basket for him and caulked it with bitumen and pitch. She put the child into it and placed it among the reeds by the bank of the Nile. And his sister stationed herself at a distance, to learn what would befall him. The daughter of Pharaoh came down to bathe in the Nile, while her maidens walked along the Nile. She spied the basket among the reeds and sent her slave girl to fetch it. When she opened it, she saw that it was a child, a boy crying. She took pity on it and said, 'This must be a Hebrew child.' Then his sister said to Pharaoh's daughter, 'Shall I go and get you a Hebrew nurse to suckle the child for you?' And Pharaoh's daughter said to her, 'Take this child and nurse it for me, and I will pay your wages.' So the woman took the child and nursed it. When the child grew up, she brought him to Pharaoh's daughter, who made him her son. She named him Moses, explaining, 'I drew him out of the water.'"

Tanakh, Torah, Exodus 2:1-10, Jewish Publication Society, 1888 (Judaism)

Auspicious Experience of the Prophet Moses

"Now, Moses, tending the flock of his father-in-law Jethero, the priest of Midian, drove the flock into the wilderness, and came to Horeb, the mountain of

God. An angel of the LORD appeared to him in a blazing fire out of a bush. He gazed, and there was a bush all aflame, yet the bush was not consumed. Moses said, 'I must turn aside to look at this marvelous sight: why doesn't the bush burn up?' When the LORD saw that he had turned aside to look, God called to him out of the bush: 'Moses! Moses!' He answered, 'Here I am.' And He said, 'Do not come closer. Remove your sandals from your feet, for the place on which you stand is holy ground. I am,' He said, 'the God of your father, the God of Abraham, the God of Isaac, and the God of Jacob.' And Moses hid his face and was afraid to look at God."

"'And the Lord continued, 'I have marked well the plight of My people in Egypt and have heeded their outcry because of their taskmaster: yes, I am mindful of their sufferings. I have come down to rescue them from the Egyptians and to bring them out of that land to a good and spacious land, a land flowing with mild and honey, the region of the Canaanites, the Hittites, the Amorites, the Perizzites, the Hivites, and the Jebusites. Now the cry of the Israelites has reached Me; moreover, I have seen how the Egyptians oppress them. Come, therefore, I will send you to Pharaoh, and you shall free My people, the Israelites, from Egypt.'"

"But Moses said to God, 'Who am I that I should go to Pharaoh and free the Israelites from Egypt?' And He said, 'I will be with you; that shall be your sign that it was I who sent you. And when you have freed the people from Egypt, you shall worship God at this mountain.'"

"Moses said to God, 'When I come to the Israelites and say to them 'The God of your fathers has sent me to you,' and they ask me, 'What is his name?' what shall I say to them?' And God said to Moses, 'Ehyeh-Asher-Ehyeh.' He continued, 'Thus shall you say to the Israelites, 'Ehyeh sent me to you.' And God said further to Moses, 'Thus shall you speak to the Israelites: The LORD, the God of your fathers, the God of Abraham, the God of Isaac, and the God of Jacob, has sent me to you: This shall be My name forever, This My appellation for all eternity.'"

"'Go and assemble the elders of Israel and say to them: the LORD, the God of your fathers, the God of Abraham, Isaac, and Jacob, has appeared to me and said, 'I have taken note of you and of what is being done to you in Egypt, and I have declared: I will take you out of the misery of Egypt to the land of the Canaanites, the Hittites, the Amorites, the Perizzites, the Hivites, and the Jebusites, to a land flowing with milk and honey.' The will listen to you: then you shall go with the elders of Israel to the king of Egypt and you shall say to him, 'The LORD, the God of the Hebrews, manifested Himself to us. Now therefore, let us go a distance of three days into the wilderness to sacrifice to the LORD our God.' Yet I know that the king of Egypt will let you go only because of a greater might. So I will stretch out My hand and smite Egypt with curious wonders which I will work upon them: after that he shall let you go. And I will dispose the Egyptians favorably toward this people, so that when you go, you will not go away empty-handed. Each woman shall borrow from her neighbor and the lodger in her house objects of silver and gold, and clothing, and you shall put these on your sons and daughters, thus stripping the Egyptians.'"

"But Moses spoke up and said, 'What if they do not believe me and do not listen to me, but say: The LORD did not appear to you?' The LORD said to him, 'What is that in your hand?' And he replied, 'A rod.' He said, 'Cast it on the ground.' He cast it on the ground and it became a snake; and Moses recoiled from it. Then the LORD said to Moses, 'Put out your hand and grasp it by the tail'- he put out his hand and seized it, and it became a rod in his hand- 'that they may believe that the LORD, the God of their fathers, the God of Abraham, the God of Isaac, and the God of Jacob, did appear to you.'"

"The LORD said to him further, 'Put your hand into your bosom.' He put his hand into his bosom; and when he took it out, his hand was encrusted with snowy scales!' And He said, 'Put your hand back into your bosom.' He put his hand back into his bosom; and when he took it out of his bosom, there it was again like the rest of his body. 'And if they do not believe you or pay heed to the first sign, they will believe the second. And if they are not convinced by both these signs and still do not heed you, take some water from the Nile and pour it on the dry ground, and it - the water that you take from the Nile - will turn to blood on the dry ground.'"

"But Moses said to the LORD, 'Please, O Lord, I have never been a man of words, either in times past or now that You have spoken to Your servant; I am slow of speech and slow of tongue.' And the LORD said to him, 'Who gives man speech? Who makes him dumb or deaf, seeing or blind? Is it not I, the LORD? Now go, and I will be with you as you speak and will instruct you what to say.' But he said, 'Please, O LORD, make someone else your agent.' The LORD became angry with Moses and He said, 'There is your brother Aaron the Levite. He, I know, speaks readily. Even now he is setting out to meet you, and he will be happy to see you. You shall speak to him and put the words in his mouth - I will with you and with him as you speak, and tell both of you what to do - and he shall speak for you to the people. Thus he shall serve as your spokesman, with you playing the role of God to him, and take with you this rod, with which you shall perform the signs.'"

"Moses went back to his father-in-law Jethero and said to him, 'Let me go back to my kinsmen in Egypt and see how they are faring.' And Jethero said to Moses, 'Go in peace.'"

"The LORD said to Moses in Midian, 'Go back to Egypt, for all the men who sought to kill you are dead.' So Moses took his wife and sons, mounted them on an ass, and went back to the land of Egypt; and Moses took the rod of God with him."
Tanakh, Torah, Exodus 3, 4:1-20, Publication Society, 1888 (Judaism)

Auspicious Death of the Prophet Moses

"Moses went up from the steppes of Moab to Mount Nebo, to the summit of Pisgah, opposite

Jericho, and the LORD showed him the whole land: Gilead as far as Dan; All Naphtali; the land of Ephraim and Manasseh; the whole land of Judah as far as the Western Sea; the Negeb; and the Plain - the Valley of Jericho, the city of palm trees - as far as Zoar. And the LORD said to him, 'This is the land of which I swore to Abraham, Isaac, and Jacob, 'I will assign it to your offspring.' I have let you see it with your own eyes, but you shall not cross there.'"

"So Moses the servant of the LORD died there, in the land of Moab, at the command of the LORD. He buried him in the valley in the land of Moab, near Beth-peor; and no one knows his burial place to this day. Moses was a hundred and twenty years old when he died; his eyes were undimmed and his vigor unabated. And the Israelites bewailed Moses in the steppes of Moab for thirty days."

"The period of wailing and mourning for Moses came to an end. Now Joshua son of Nun was filled with the spirit of wisdom because Moses had laid his hands upon him; and the Israelites heeded him, doing as the LORD had commanded Moses."

Tanakh, Torah, Deuteronomy 34:1-9, Publication Society, 1888 (Judaism)

Auspicious Experience of the Prophet Isaiah

"The vision which Isaiah, son of Amoz, had concerning Judah and Jerusalem . . . 'Hear, O heavens, and listen, O earth for the LORD speaks: . . . 'Put away your misdeeds from before my eyes; cease

doing evil; learn to do good. Make justice your aim: redress for the wronged, hear the orphan's plea, defend the widow. Come now, let us set things right, says the Lord: Though your sins be like scarlet, they may become white as snow; though they be crimson red, they may become white as wool. If you are willing, and obey, you shall eat the good things of the land; but if you refuse and resist, the sword shall consume you: for the mouth of the Lord has spoken!'"
New American Bible, Old Testament, Isaiah, 1: 1, 2, 1:16-20, (Judaism, Christianity)

Death According to the Prophet Isaiah

"Seek the Lord while He can be found,
Call to Him while He is near.
Let the wicked give up his ways,
The sinful man his plans;
Let him turn back to the LORD,
And He will pardon him;
To our God,
For he freely forgives.
For My plans are not your plans,
Nor are my ways your ways
- declares the LORD.
But as the heavens are high above the earth,
So are My ways high above your ways,
And My plans above your plans.
For as the rains or snow drops from heaven
And returns not there,
But soaks the earth

And makes it bring forth vegetation,
Yielding seed for sowing and bread for eating,
So is the word that issues from My mouth:
It does not come back to Me unfulfilled,
But performs what I purpose,
Achieves what I sent it to do.
Yea, you shall leave in joy and be lead home secure.
Before you, mount and hill shall shout aloud,
And all the trees of the field shall clap their hands.
Instead of the brier, a cypress shall rise;
Instead of the nettle, a myrtle shall rise.
These shall stand as a testimony to the Lord,
As an everlasting sign that shall not perish."
Tanakh, Nevi'im, Isaiah 55:6-13, 56:1, Jewish
Publication Society, 1888, (Judaism)

Death According to the Talmud

"When the time came for Rabbi Hiyya to die, the Angel of Death could not approach him. The Angel disguised himself as a beggar, and knocked at the door of Rabbi Hiyya. The Rabbi gave him some bread, and the supposed beggar said: 'You pity me as a beggar; why dost thou not pity me as a Messenger of God, commissioned to bring thee before Him?' The rabbi gave up his soul without further protest."
The Talmudic Anthology, No. 56, The Dead, Alms for
the Angel of Death, Moed Katon, 28, Edited by Louis
J. Newman, Behrman House, Inc. 1945, (Judaism)

"Some say that the Kaddish for a son who

mourns his parent originated in this way. A Tanna dreamed he was walking in a deserted place and encountered a spirit loaded with wood. Answering his inquiry, the spirit said that he had been sentenced to carry the wood to Gehenna for a heinous sin he had committed. 'Is there any way I can help you?' asked the Rabbi. 'Yes, I left a young son in this town (and he named it), and his name is (and he gave the name). If he should go to the synagogue and declare in public a recitation of praise unto the Lord, my sin will be remitted.' The Tanna searched for and discovered the son, and since he knew no Hebrew, he taught the boy the Kaddish in a mixed Hebrew and Aramaic."

The Talmudic Anthology, No.61, Death and Mourning, The Origin of the Mourner's Kaddish, Midrash on the Decalogue, Edited by Louis J. Newman, Behrman House, Inc. 1945, (Judaism)

"R. Abba asked R. Judah: 'We are taught that the Torah was inscribed on High long before man was created. And in the Torah it is written that man shall die, whether he be just or wicked. Is there no difference between the good and the evil in this world?' R. Judah answered: 'We cannot know the ways of God, but perhaps we may discover a difference. Had man been perfect in everything he did, he might never have died, but would merely have been summoned to Heaven alive, as was Elijah."

The Talmudic Anthology, No. 56, The Dead, Must Man Die?, Zohar, iii, 159, Edited by Louis J. Newman, Behrman House, Inc. 1945, (Judaism)

Death According to the Zohar

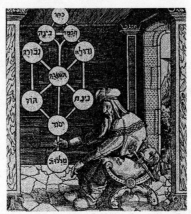

Jewish Kabbalist Holding the Ten Sephirot
(*"My Jewish World," By Rabbi Dr. Raphael Posner, Volume 4, Page 7, Joseph Ben Braham Gikatilla - Artist, Encyclopaedia Judaica, 1975*)

"And the Lord spoke unto Moses, saying: Speak unto Aaron, and say unto him: When thou lightest the lamps . . . . R. Judah discoursed here on the verse: 'Which is as a bridegroom coming out of his chamber', etc. (Ps. xixi, 6). 'Happy is the portion of Israel', he said, 'in whom the Holy One, blessed be He, delights and to whom He gave the Torah of truth, the Tree of Life, whoever takes hold of which achieves life in this world and in the world to come. Now the Tree of Life extends from above downward and it is the Sun which illumines all. Its radiance commences at the top and extends through the whole trunk in a straight line. It is composed of two sides, one to the north, one to the south, one to the right, and one to the left. When the trunk shines, first the right arm of the tree is illumined, and from its intensity the left side catches the light. The 'chamber' from which he goes forth is the starting-point of light, referred to also in the words of the next verse, 'from the end of the heaven', which is, indeed, the starting-point of all."

The Zohar, Volume V, Baha'Alothekha, Number VIII, I-XII, 16, Page 203, Translated by Harry Sperling and Maurice Simon, Soncino Press, 1984, (Judaism)

Auspicious Experience of the Prophet Abraham

Abraham
(Tradition purports him to have written Sepher Yezirah) (*"The Book of Life"*, *By Newton Marshall Hall and Irving Francis Wood, Volume 2, Page 34, Edwin John Prittie - Artist, John Rudin & Co., Inc, 1923*)

"The LORD appeared to him by the terebinths of Mamre; he was sitting at the entrance of the tent as the day grew hot. Looking up, he saw three men standing near him. As soon as he saw them, he ran from the entrance of the tent to greet them and, bowing to the ground, he said, 'My lords, if it please you, do not go on past your servant. Let a little water be brought; bathe your feet and recline under the tree. And let me fetch a morsel of bread that you may refresh yourselves; then go on - seeing that you have come your servant's way.' They replied, 'Do as you have said.'"

"Abraham hastened into the tent to Sarah, and

said, 'Quick, three seahs of choice flour! Knead and make cakes!' Then Abraham ran to the herd, took a calf, tender and choice, and gave it to a servant-boy, who hastened to prepare it. He took curds and milk and the calf that had been prepared and set these before them; and he waited on them under the tree as they ate."

"They said to him, 'Where is your wife Sarah?' And he replied, 'There in the tent.' Then one said, 'I will return to you next year, and your wife Sarah shall have a son! . . . Is anything too wondrous for the LORD?'"

Tanakh, Torah, Genesis 18:1-15, Jewish Publication Society, 1982, (Judaism)

Auspicious Words of the Prophet Abraham

"Yah, the Lord of hosts, the living God, King of the Universe, Omnipotent, All-Kind and Merciful, Supreme and Extolled, who is Eternal, Sublime and Most-Holy, ordained (formed) and created the Universe in thirty-two mysterious paths of wisdom by three Sepharim . . ."

Sepher Yezirah, Chapter 1, Section 1, Translated by Rev. Dr. Isidor Kalisch, L.H. Frank & Co., 1877, (Judaism)

Auspicious Birth and 'Taking Up' of the Prophet Enoch

'Head of a Patriarch' (Enoch)
(*"The Law and the Prophets," Giovanni Battista Tiepolo - Artist, Page 355, Art Institute of Chicago, Harry N. Abrams, Inc.*)

"When Jared was a hundred and sixty-two years old he fathered Enoch . . . When Enoch was sixty-five years old he fathered Methuselah. Enoch walked with God. After the birth of Methuselah, Enoch lived for three hundred years . . . Enoch walked with God, then was no more, because God took him."
The New Jerusalem Bible, Genesis 5:18-24, Doubleday, 1985 (Judaism)

Auspicious Experience of the Prophet Enoch

"There my eyes beheld all who, without sleeping, stand before him and bless him, saying, Blessed be thou, and blessed be the name of God for ever and for ever. Then my countenance became changed, until I was incapable of seeing."

"After this I beheld thousands of thousands, and myriads of myriads, and an infinite number of people, standing before the Lord of spirits."

"On the four wings likewise of the Lord of spirits, on the four sides, I perceived others, besides those who were standing *before him*. Their names, too, I know; because the angel, who proceeded with me, declared them to me, discovering to me every secret thing."

"Then I heard the voices of those upon the four sides magnifying the Lord of glory."

"The first voice blessed the Lord of spirits for ever and for ever."

"The second voice I heard blessing the elect One, and the elect who suffer on account of the Lord of spirits."

"The third voice I heard petitioning and praying for those who dwell upon earth, and supplicate the name of the Lord of spirits."

"The fourth voice I heard expelling the impious angels, and prohibiting them from entering into presence of the Lord of spirits, to prefer accusations against the inhabitants of the earth."

"After this I besought the angel of peace, who proceeded with me, to explain all that was concealed. I said to him, Who are those *whom I* have seen on the four sides, and whose words I have heard and written down? He replied, the first is the merciful, the patient, the holy Michael."

"The second is he who *presides* over all that is

powerful, is Gabriel. And the fourth, who *presides* over repentance, and the hope of those who will inherit eternal life, is Phanuel. These are the four angels of the most high God, and their four voices, which at that time I heard."

The Book of Enoch, Chapter XXXIX, No. 12, Chapter XL, No. 1-9, Chapter XLI, No. 1, Wizards Bookshelf, 1983, (Judaism)

Auspicious Experience of the Prophet Ezekiel

'The Jewish Rabbi'
("The Law and the Prophets," Rembrandt - Artist, Page 218, The National Gallery in London, Harry N. Abrams, Inc.)

"In the thirtieth year, on the fifth day of the fourth month, as I was among the exiles by the River Chebar, heaven opened and I saw visions from God. on the fifth of the month - it was the fifth year of exile for King Jehoiachin - the word of Yahweh was addressed to the priest Ezekiel son of Buzi, in Chaldaea by the River Chebar. There the hand of Yahweh came on him."

"I looked; a stormy wind blew form the north, a great cloud with flashing fire and brilliant light round it, and in the middle, in the heart of the fire, a brilliance like that of amber, and in the middle what seemed to be four living creatures. They looked like this: They were of human form. Each had four faces, each had four wings. Their legs were straight; they had hooves like calves, glittering like polished brass.

Below their wings, they had human hands on all four sides corresponding to their four faces and four wings. They touched one another with their wings; they did not turn as they moved; each one moved straight forward. As to the appearance of their faces, all four had a human face, and a lion's face to the right, and all four had a bull's face to the left and all four had an eagle's face. Their wings were spread upwards, each had one pair touching its neighbor's, and the other pair covering its body. And each one moved straight forward; they went where the spirit urged them, they did not turn as they moved."

"Between these living creatures were what looked like blazing coals, like torches, darting backward and forwards between the living creatures; the fired gave a brilliant light, and lightning flashed from the fire, and the living creatures kept disappearing and reappearing like flashes of lightning."

"Now, as I looked at the living creatures, I saw a wheel toughing the ground beside each of the four-faced living creatures. The appearance and structure of the wheels were like glittering chrysolite. All four looked alike, and their appearance and structure were such that each wheel seemed to have another wheel inside it. In whichever of the four directions they moved, they did not need to turn as they moved. Their circumference was of awe-inspiring size, and the rims of all four sparkled all the way round. When the living creatures moved, the wheels moved beside them; and when the living creatures left the ground, the wheels too left the ground. They moved in whichever direction the spirit chose to go, and the wheels rose with them, since the wheels shared the spirit of the animals. When the living creatures moved on, they moved on; when the former halted the latter halted; when the former left the ground, the wheels too left the ground, since the wheels shared the spirit of the animals. Over the heads of the living creatures was what looked like a solid surface glittering like crystal, spread out over their heads, above them, and under the solid surface, their wings were spread out straight, touching one another, and each had a pair covering its body. I also heard the noise of their wings; when they moved, it was like the noise of flood-waters, like the voice of Shaddai, like the noise of a storm, like the noise of an armed camp; and when they halted, they lowered their wings; there was a noise, too."

"Beyond the solid surface above their heads, there was what seemed like a sapphire, in the form of a throne. High above on the form of a throne was a form with the appearance of a human being."

"I saw a brilliance like amber, like fire, radiating from what appeared to be the waist upwards; and from what appeared to be the waist downwards, I saw what looked like fire, giving brilliant light all round. The radiance of the encircling light was like the radiance of the bow in the clouds on rainy days. The sight was like the glory of Yahweh. I looked and fell to the ground, and I heard the voice of someone speaking to me."

"He said, 'Son of man, get to your feet; I will speak to you.' As he said these words the spirit came into me and put me on my feet, and I heard him speaking to me. He said, 'Son of man, I am sending you to the Israelites, to the rebels who have rebelled against me. They and their ancestors have been in revolt against me up to the present day. Because they are stubborn and obstinate children, I am sending them, to say, 'Lord Yahweh says this.' Whether they listen or not, this tribe of rebels will know there is a prophet among them. And you, son of man, do not be afraid of them or of what they say, though you find yourself surrounded with brambles and sitting on scorpions. Do not be afraid of their words or alarmed by their looks, for they are a tribe of rebels. You are to deliver my words to them whether they listen or not, for they are a tribe of rebels. But you, son of man, are to listen to what I say to you; do not be a rebel like that rebellious tribe. Open your mouth and eat what I am about to give to you."

"When I looked, there was a hand stretching out to me, holding a scroll. He unrolled it in front of me; it was written on, front and back; on it was written 'Lamentations, dirges and cries of grief.'"

"He then said, 'Son of man, eat what you see; eat this scroll, then go and speak to the House of Israel. I opened my mouth; he gave me the scroll to eat and then said, 'Son of man, feed on this scroll which I am giving you and eat your fill.' So I ate it and it tasted sweet as honey."

"He then said, 'Son of man, go to the House of Israel and tell them what I have said.'"

The New Jerusalem Bible, Ezekiel 1, 2, 3:1-6,
Doubleday, 1985 (Judaism)

Auspicious Experience of Job

Job

("The Book of Life," By Newton Marshall Hall and Irving Francis Wood, Volume 5, Page 288, Helen Bennett - Artist, John Rudin and Co., 1923)

"Job said in reply to the Lord:
'I know that You can do everything,
That nothing you propose is impossible for You.
Who is this who obscures counsel without knowledge?
Indeed, I spoke without understanding
Of things beyond me, which I did not know.
Hear now, and I will speak;
I will ask, and You will inform me.
I had heard You with my ears,
But now I see You with my eyes;
Therefore, I recant and relent,
Being but dust and ashes."
Tanakh, Kethuvim, Job 42:1-6, Jewish Publication Society, 1982, (Judaism)

Auspicious Words of Spinoza

Spinoza

("My Jewish World," Volume 6, Page 3, By Rabbi Dr. Raphael Posner, Encyclopaedica Judaica, 1975)

"Every man's true happiness and blessedness consist solely in the enjoyment of what is good, not in the pride that he alone is enjoying it, to the exclusion of others. He who thinks himself the more blessed because he is enjoying benefits which others are not, or because he is more blessed or more fortunate than his fellows, is ignorant of true happiness and blessedness, and the joy which he feels is either childish or envious and malicious. For instance, a man's true happiness consists only in wisdom, and the knowledge of the truth, not at all in the fact that he is wiser than others, or that others lack such knowledge: such considerations do not increase his wisdom or true happiness."

Works of Spinoza, Volume 1, Translated by R.H.M. Elwes, Dover Publications, 1951, (Judaism: Philosophy)

CHAPTER THREE
MYSTERY RELIGION

Thoth   **Hermes**

*("Lexicon Universal Encyclopedia, From the Tomb of Ramses I,
Volume 7, Page 84, Lexicon Publications 1987) AND ("The Divine
Pymander of Hermes," Translated by Dr. Everard, Cover, Wizard
Books, 1978)*

Nefertiti

*("Tutankhamen," By E. Wallis Budge, Page ii, Limestone Head in the
Museum at Berlin, Bell Publishing Co., 1923)*

Auspicious Birth of Thoth/Hermes the Prophet (Who are Considered Different Incarnations of the Same Prophet)

The Prophet Thoth/Hermes is said to have been born and reborn for thousands of years beginning about 4,000 years ago in Ancient Egypt. It is not known at what age Thoth/Hermes were at the time they received their call.

Queen Nefertiti was so adored that she ended up being venerated as somewhat of a 'holy mother.' Not unlike Isis (The more greatly venerated Holy Mother) and Osiris (The Egyptian Saviour). Husband and wife, Osiris is mythologized to have been raised from the dead after being cut into many pieces.

"I, Thoth, the Atlantean, master of mysteries, keeper of records, mighty king, magician, living from generation to generation, being about to pass into the Halls of Amenti, set down for the guidance of those that are to come after, these records of the mighty wisdom of Great Atlantis."

"In the great city of KEOR, on the island of UNDAL, in a time of far past, I began this incarnation; not as the little men of the present age did the mighty ones of Atlantis live and die but rather from aeon to aeon, did they renew their life in the Halls of Amenti, where the river of life flows eternally onward."

"A hundred times ten have I descended the dark way that led into light, and as many times have I ascended from the darkness into the light, my strength and power renewed."

"Now for a time I descend and the men of KHEM shall know me no more, but in a time yet unborn will I rise again, mighty and potent, requiring an accounting of those left behind me."

The Emerald Tablets of Thoth the Atlantean, Tablet I, Page 7, Paragraphs 1-3, Translated by Doral, Brother of the White Temple, 1939, (Mystery Religions, Words of Thoth)

Auspicious Experience of Thoth/Hermes the Prophet (Who are Considered Different Incarnations of the Same Prophet)

"Far into space my SOUL traveled freely, into infinity's circle of light. Strange, beyond knowledge, were some of the planets, great and gigantic, beyond dreams of men. Yet found I law, in all of its beauty, working through and among them, as here among men. Flashed forth my Soul through infinity's beauty, far through space I flew with my thoughts."

"Rested I there on a planet of beauty, strains of harmony filled all the air; shapes there were, moving in order, great and majestic as stars in the night; mounting in harmony, ordered equilibrium, symbols of the Cosmic, like unto law."

"Many the stars I passed in my journey, many the races of men on their worlds; some reaching high as stars of the morning, some falling low in the blackness of night. Each and all of them struggling

54

upward, gaining the heights and plumbing the depths, moving at times in realms of brightness, living through darkness, gaining the Light."

"Know, O man, that light is thine heritage, know that darkness is only a veil, Sealed in thine heart is brightness eternal, waiting the moment of freedom to conquer, waiting to rend the veil of the night."

The Emerald Tablets of Thoth the Atlantean, Tablet IV, Page 7, The Space Born, Page 23-24, Translated by Doral, Brother of the White Temple, 1939, (Mystery Religions, Words of Thoth)

Auspicious Death of Thoth/Hermes the Prophet (Who are Considered Different Incarnations of the Same Prophet)

"Emissary on earth am I of the Dweller, fulfilling his commands so man might be lifted. Now return I to the Halls of Amenti, leaving behind me some of my wisdom. Preserve ye and keep ye the command of the Dweller, lift ever upwards your eyes toward the light. Surely in time, ye are one with the Master, surely by right ye are one with the Master, surely by right ye are one with the ALL."

"Now, I depart from ye, know my commandments, keep them and be them, and I will be with you, helping and guiding you into the Light."

"Now before me opens the portal, go I down in the darkness of night."

The Emerald Tablets of Thoth the Atlantean, Tablet I,
Page10, Translated by Doral, Brother of the White
Temple, 1939, (Mystery Religions, Words of Thoth)

Death According to the Prophet Thoth/Hermes (Who are Considered Different Incarnations of the Same Prophet)

"But the Soul of Man, and yet not everyone, but that which is pious and religious, is Angelic and Divine. And such a soul, after it is departed from the body, having striven the strife of Piety, becomes either Mind or God."

"And the strife of piety is to know God, and to injure no Man; and this way it becomes Mind.

"But the impious Soul abideth in its own offence, punished of itself, and seeking an earthly and humane body to enter into."

For no other Body is capable of a Humane soul, neither is it lawful for a Man's Soul to fall into the Body of an unreasonable living thing: For it is the Law or Decree of God to preserve a Human Soul from so great a contumely and reproach.

"Tat. How then is the Soul of Man punished, O Father, and what is its greatest torment?"

"Herm. Impiety, O my Son; for what Fire has so great a flame as it? Or what biting Beast doth so tear the Body as it doth the Soul?"

"Or dost thou not see how many Evils the wicked soul suffereth, roaring and crying out, I am burned, I am consumed, I know not what to say or do, I am devoured, unhappy wretch, of the evils that compass and lay hold upon me; miserable that I am, I neither hear nor see anything."

"These are the voices of a punished and tormented Soul, and not as many; and thou, O Son, thinkest that the Soul going out of the Body grows brutish or enters into a Beast: which is a very great error, for the Soul punished after this manner."

"For the Mind, when it is ordered or appointed to get a Fiery Body for the services of God, coming down into the wicked soul, torments it with the sips of Sins, wherewith the wicked Soul, being scourged, turns itself to Murders and Contumelies, and Blasphemies, and divers violences, and other things by which men are injured."

"But into a pious soul, the mind entering, leads it into the Light of Knowledge . . . Therefore, O Son, we must give thanks and pray that we may obtain a good mind."

" . . . Tat. And wherefore, Father?"

"Trism. Know, Son, that every Soul hath the Good Mind; for of that it is we now speak, and not of that Minister of whom we said before, that he was sent from the Judgment."

"For the Soul without the Mind can neither say nor do anything; for many times the Mind flies away from the Soul, and in that hour the Soul neither seeth nor heareth, but is like an unreasonable thing; so great is the power of the Mind."

"But neither brooketh it an idle or lazy Soul, but leaves such an one fastened to the Body, and by it is pressed down."

"And such a Soul, O Son, hath no Mind; wherefore neither must such a one be called a Man."

"For Man is a Divine living thing, and is not to be compared to any brute Beast that lives upon Earth, but to them that are above in Heaven . . ."

"Rather, if we shall be bold to speak the truth, he that is a Man indeed is above them, or at least they are equal in power, one to the other. For none of the things in Heaven will come down upon Earth, and leave the limits of Heaven, but a Man ascends up into Heaven, and measures it."

"And he knoweth what things are on high, and what below, and learneth all other things exactly."

The Divine Pymander of Hermes, The Fourth Book, 64-76, 85-92, Translated by Dr. Everard, Wizards Bookshelf, 1985, (Hermetic, Words of Hermes)

Auspicious Words of the Prophet Pythagorus

Pythagoras

("The Pythagorean Sourcebook and Library," Compiled/Translated by Kenneth Sylvan Guthrie, Cover, Phanes Press, 1987)

"The principles of all virtue are three: knowledge, power and deliberate choice. Knowledge indeed is that by which we contemplate and form a judgment of things; power is a certain strength of nature from which we derive our subsistence, and which gives stability to our actions; and deliberate choice is, as it were, the hand of the soul by which we are impelled to, and lay hold on, the objects of our choice."

"The soul is divided into reasoning power, anger and desire. Reasoning power rules knowledge, anger deals with impulse, and desire bravely rules the soul's affections. When these three parts unite into one action, exhibiting a composite energy, then concord and virtue result in the soul. When sedition divides them, then discord and vice appear."

The Pythagorean Sourcebook and Library, Theages:

On the Virtues, Page 226, Compiled by Kenneth Sylvan Guthrie, Phanes Press, 1987, (Mystery Religions: Pythagorean)

Auspicious Experience of Louis Claude de St. Martin

Louis Claude de St. Martin
(The Unknown Philosopher, By Arthur Edward Waite, Rudolf Steiner Publications, 1970)

"A few days after I beheld very plainly in front of me, close at hand, our Divine Master, Jesus Christ, crucified on the tree of the cross. Again, after another interval, this same Divine Master appeared to me, but this time as He came forth from the tomb wherein His body had been laid. Lastly, after a third interval, our Divine Master Jesus Christ appeared to me, all glorious and triumphant over the world and over Satan with his pomps, passing in front of me with the Blessed Virgin Mary, His mother, and followed by a number of persons."

The Unknown Philosopher, In the Occult World, Page 42, By Arthur Edward Waite, Rudolf Steiner Publications, 1970, (Mystery Religions, Words of Louis Claude de St. Martin)

CHAPTER FOUR
ZOROASTRIANISM

Zarathustra
("Religions of the World," Reconstruction by D.F. Karaka, Page 59,
From the Bettman Archives, St. Martin's Press, 1993)

Auspicious Birth of the Prophet Zarathustra

The Prophet Zarathustra is said to have been born around the 630 B.C.E., born in Rhages, a town near present day Tehran, Iran. Zarathustra received his call when he was 30 years of age.

"The third of five sons in a family of poor warriors, he showed a religious bent and was trained to conduct sacrifices and intone sacred chants. At the age of 20 he left his parents' home to meditate in the mountains."
Religions of the World, Third Edition, Religions of

Antiquity, Zoroastrianism, Page 60, St. Martin's Press, 1993, Group of Writers

"Zarathustra was born in the House of Pourushaspa upon the mountains beside the river Darega. In symbols this tells us that 'the ideal worship' is 'born' in the household 'possessing excellence' in an 'environment' built upon 'mountains' (that is, on spiritual mental, and physical heights) as they are found to stand beside 'the river of the long tradition teaching,' mentioned in Yast 11:17, 22."

Avestan Symbols and Concepts, Chapter 5, Page 57, Translated and Published by Reverend Ernestine G. Busch, (Zoroastrianism)

"Legendary material states that demons attempted to kill the infant Zoroaster several times because they recognized him as a potential enemy.'They rush away shouting, the wicked, evil-doing Daevas; they run away shouting, the wicked, evil-doing Daevas; 'Let us gather together at the head of Aresura! For he is just born, the holy Zoroaster, in the house of Proushaspa. How can we procure his death? He is the weapon that fells the friends; he is a Druj to the Druj!' Vanished are the Daeva-worshipers, the Nasu made by the Daevas, the false speaking lie.' Each attempt on the infant's life was thwarted by the powers that watched over him."

Religions of the World, Third Edition, Zoroastrianism, The Life of Zoroaster, Page 248, Prentice Hall, 1994, (Collection)

Auspicious Experiences of the Prophet Zarathustra

"When he was 30 years old - a significant age for many spiritual leaders - he had his first vision."

"Zarathustra was freed from his material body and raised up to the court of heaven. There Ahura Mazda revealed that he was opposed by Aura Mainyu, the spirit and promoter of evil, and charged Zarathustra with the task of calling all human beings to choose between him (good) and Aura Mainyu (evil). The prophet continued to receive revelations from six archangels whom he regarded as aspects of Ahura Mazda. Zarathustra's God remained a mighty, somewhat abstract being: 'He that in the beginning thus thought, 'Let the blessed realms be filled with lights,' he it is that by his wisdom created Right . . . I conceived of thee, O Mazda, in my thought that thou, the First, art (also) the Last, that thou art father of Good Thought . . . and art the Lord to judge the actions of life.'"

"Partly as a result of this vision, the prophet enjoined his listeners to lead ethical lives under the direction of Good Thought."

Religions of the World, Third Edition, Religions of Antiquity, Zoroastrianism, Page 60, St. Martin's Press, 1993, Group of Writers

"The sage asked the spirit of wisdom thus: 'How is it possible to seek the maintenance and prosperity of the body without injury of the soul, and the preservation of the soul without injury of the body?' The spirit of wisdom answered thus: 'Him who is less than thee consider as an equal, and an equal as a superior, and a greater than him as a chieftain, and a chieftain as a ruler. And among rulers one is to be acquiescent, obedient and true-speaking; and among accusers (or associates) be submissive, mild, and kindly regardful . . ."

"Commit no slander . . . Form no covetous desire . . . Indulge in no wrathfulness . . . Suffer no anxiety . . . Commit no lustfulness . . . Bear no improper envy . . . Commit no sin on account of disgrace . . . Practice no sloth . . . Choose a wife who is of character . . . Commit no unseasonable chatter . . . Commit no running about uncovered . . . Thou shouldst be diligent and moderate . . . Do not extort from the wealth of others . . . Thou shouldst be an abstainer from the wives of others . . . With enemies fight with equity . . . With a friend proceed with the approval of friends . . . With a malicious man carry on no conflict . . . "

The Pahlavi Texts, Menog-i Khrad, Chapter 2, 1-56
(Zoroastrianism)

Auspicious Death of the Prophet Zarathustra

"During a war with the Turanians, the city in which Zoroaster lived was invaded. An enemy soldier found the seventy-seven-year-old prophet tending the sacred flame in the fire temple and killed him."

Religions of the World, Third Edition,
Zoroastrianism, The Life of Zoroaster, Page 249,

Prentice Hall, 1994, (Collection)

Death According to the Prophet Zarathustra

"The twenty-third question is that which you ask thus: When he who is righteous passes away, where is the place the soul sits the first night, the second, and the third; and what does it do? The reply is this, that thus it is said, that the soul of man, itself the spirit of the body, after passing away, is three nights upon earth, doubtful about its own position (gas), and in fear of the account; and it experiences terror, distress (dahyako), and fear through anxiety about the Chinwad bridge; and as it sits it notices about its own good works and sin. And the soul, which in a manner belongs to that same spirit of the body which is alike experiencing and alike touching it, becomes acquainted by sight with the sin which it has committed, and the good works which it has scantily done. And the first night from its own good thoughts, the second night from its good words, and the third night from its good deeds it obtains pleasure for the soul; and if also, with the righteousness there be sin which remains in it as its origin, the first punishment in retribution for the evil deed occurs that same third night. The same third night, on the fresh arrival of a dawn, the treasurer of good works, like a handsome maiden (kaniko), comes out to meet it with the store of its own good works; and, collected by witches (pariko-chind), the sin and crime unatoned for (atokhto) come on to the account and are justly

accounted for. For the remaining (ketrund) sin it
undergoes punishment at the (chinwad) bridge, and
the evil thoughts, evil words, and evil deeds are
atoned for; and with the good thoughts, good words,
and good deeds of its own commendable and
pleasing spirit it steps forward unto the supreme
heaven (garothman), or to heaven (vahishto), or to the
ever-stationary (hamistagan) [purgatory] of the
righteous, there where there is a place for it in
righteousness."
*Pahlavi Texts, Dadestan- i Denig, Chapter 24, 1-6,
(Zoroastrianism)*

"Thou shouldst not become presumptuous
through life; for death comes upon thee at last, the
dog and the bird lacerate the corpse, and the
perishable part (sejinako) falls to the ground. During
three days and nights the soul sits at the crown of the
head of the body. And the fourth day, in the light of
dawn with the cooperation of Srosh the righteous,
Vae the good, and Warharan the strong, the
opposition of Astwihad, Vae the bad, Frazishto the
demon, and Nizishto the demon, and the evil-
designing action of Eshm, the evil-doer, the
impetuous assailant it goes up to the awful, lofty
Chinwad bridge, to which every one, righteous and
wicked, is coming. And many opponents have
watched there, with the desire of evil of Eshm, the
impetuous assailant, and of Astwihad who devours
creatures of every kind and knows no satiety, and the
mediation of Mihr and Srosh and Rashn, and the
weighing of Rashn, the just, with the balance of the

spirits, which renders no favor (hu-girai) on any side, neither for the righteous nor yet the wicked, neither for the lords nor yet the monarchs. As much as a hair's breadth it will not turn, and has no partiality; and he who is a lord and monarch it considers equally, in its decision, with him who is the least of mankind."

"And when a soul of the righteous passes upon that bridge, the width of the bridge becomes as it were a league (parasang), and the righteous soul passes over with the cooperation of Srosh the righteous. And his own deeds of a virtuous kind come to meet him in the form of a maiden, who is handsomer and better than every maiden in the world."

"And the righteous soul speaks thus: 'Who mayest thou be, that a maiden who is handsomer and better than thee was never seen by me in the worldly existence?' In reply that maiden form responds thus: 'I am no maiden, but I am thy virtuous deeds, thou youth who art well-thinking, well-speaking, well-doing, and of good religion! For when thou sawest in the world him who performed demon-worship, then thou hast sat down, and thy performance was the worship of the sacred beings. And when it was seen by thee that there was any one who caused oppression and plunder, and distressed or scorned a good person, and acquired wealth by crime, then thou keptest back from the creatures their own risk of oppression and plunder; the good person was also thought of by thee, and lodging and entertainment provided; and alms were given by thee to him who came forth from near and him, too, who was from afar; and wealth which was due to honesty was acquired by thee. And when thou sawest him who practiced false justice and taking of bribes, and false evidence was given by him, then thou hast sat down, and the recitation of truth and virtue was uttered by thee. I am this of thine, the good thoughts, the good words, and the good deeds which were thought and spoken and done by thee. For when I have become commendable, I am then made altogether more commendable by thee; (138) when I have become precious, I am then made altogether still more precious by thee; (139) and when I have become glorious, I am then made altogether still more glorious by thee.' And when he walks onwards from there, a sweet-scented breeze comes then to meet him, which is more fragrant than all perfume. The soul of the righteous inquires of Srosh thus: 'That breeze is this, that never in the world so fragrant a breeze came into contact with me?' Then Srosh, the righteous, replies to that righteous soul thus: 'This breeze is from heaven, which is so fragrant.'

"Afterwards, on his march, the first step is set on the place of good thoughts, the second on that of good words, the third on that of good deeds, and the fourth step reaches up unto the endless light which is all-radiant. And angels and archangels of every description come to meet him, and ask tidings from him thus: 'How hast thou come, from that which is a perishable, fearful, and very miserable existence, to this which is an imperishable existence that is undisturbed, thou youth who art well-thinking, well-speaking, well-doing, and of good religion?' Then Ohrmazd, the lord, speaks thus: 'Ask ye from him no tidings; for he has parted from that which was a precious body, and has come by that which is a fearful road. And bring ye unto him the most agreeable of eatables, that which is the mid-spring butter [Maidyozarem roghan], so that he may rest his soul from that bridge of the three nights, unto which he came from Astwihad and the remaining demons; and seat him upon an all-embellished throne.' As it is declared that: 'Unto the righteous man and woman, after passing away, they bring food of the most agreeable of eatables -- the food of the angels of the spiritual existences -- that which is the mid-spring butter; and they seat them down on an all-embellished throne. For ever and everlasting they remain in all glory with the angels of the spiritual existences everlastingly.'"

"And when he who is wicked dies, his soul then rushes about for three days and nights in the vicinity of the head of that wicked one, and sobs thus: 'Whither do I go, and now what do I make as a refuge?' And the sin and crime of every kind, that were committed by him in the worldly existence, he sees with his eyes in those three days and nights. The fourth day Vizaresh, the demon, comes and binds the soul of the wicked with the very evil noose; and with the opposition of Srosh, the righteous, he leads it up to the Chinwad bridge. Then Rashn, the just, detects that soul of the wicked through its wickedness. Afterwards, Vizaresh, the demon, takes that soul of the wicked, and mercilessly and maliciously beats and maltreats it. And that soul of the wicked weeps with a loud voice, is fundamentally horrified, implores with many supplicating entreaties, and makes many struggles for life disconnectedly. Whom -- when his struggling and supplication are of no avail whatever, and no one comes to his assistance from the divinities (bagan), nor yet from the demons -- moreover, Vizaresh, the demon, drags miserably to the inevitable hell. And then a maiden who is not like unto maidens comes to meet him. And that soul of the wicked speaks to that evil maiden thus: 'Who mayest thou be, that never in the worldly existence was an evil maiden seen by me, who was viler and more hideous than thee?' And she speaks in reply to him (171) thus: 'I am not a maiden, but I am thy deeds, thou monster who art evil-thinking, evil-speaking, evil-doing, and of evil religion! For even when thou sawest him who performed the worship of the sacred beings, still then thou hast sat down, and demon-worship was performed by thee, and the demons and fiends were served. And also when thou sawest him who provided lodging and entertainment, and gave alms, for a good person who came forth from near and him, too, who was from afar, then thou actedest scornfully and disrespectfully to the good person, and gave no alms, and even shut up the door. And when thou sawest him who practiced true justice, took no bribe, gave true evidence, and uttered virtuous recitation, even then thou hast sat down, and false justice was practiced by thee, evidence was given by thee with falsehood, and vicious recitation was uttered by thee. I am this of thine, the evil thoughts, the evil words, and the evil deeds which were thought and spoken and done by thee. For when I have become uncommendable, I am then made altogether still more uncommendable, by thee; when I have become unrespected, I am then made altogether still more unrespected by thee; and when I have sat in an eye-offending position, I am then made altogether still more really eye-offending (chashm-kah-ichtar-ich) by thee.'"

"Afterwards he enters, the first step on the place of evil thoughts, the second on that of evil words, the third step on that of evil deeds, and the fourth step rushes into the presence of the wicked evil spirit and the other demons. And the demons make ridicule and mockery of him thus: 'What was thy trouble and complaint, as regards Ohrmazd, the lord, and the archangels, and the fragrant and joyful heaven, when thou approachedest for a sight of Ahriman and the demons and gloomy hell, although we cause thee misery therein and do not pity, and thou shalt see misery of long duration?' And the evil spirit shouts to the demons thus: 'Ask ye no tidings from him who is parted from that which was a precious body, and has come on by that which is a very bad road. But bring ye unto him the foulest and vilest of eatables, the food which is nurtured in hell.' They bring the poison and venom of the snake and scorpion and other noxious creatures that are in hell, and give him to eat. And until the resurrection and future existence he must be in hell, in much misery and punishment of various kinds. Especially that it is possible to eat food there only as though by similitude.'"

"The spirit of innate wisdom spoke to the sage thus: 'This which was asked by thee, as to the maintenance of the body and concerning the preservation of the soul, is also spoken about by me, and thou art admonished. Be virtuously assiduous about it, and keep it in practice; for this is thy chief way for the maintenance of the body and preservation of the soul.'

The Pahlavi Texts, Menog-i Khrad, Chapter 2, 110-198, (Zoroastrianism)

CHAPTER FIVE
BUDDHISM

The Buddha
("The Teachings of the Compassionate Buddha," Edited by E.A. Burtt,
Cover, Mentor Religion, 1955)

Avalokiteshwara
(A Monk from Shasta Abbey, Mt. Shasta, California)

Auspicious Birth of the Prophet Buddha

The Prophet Buddha is said to have been born around 563 B.C.E. in the Northeastern Indian subcontinent to a wealthy royal family. The Buddha himself was a prince (Prince Siddhartha), the son of a king. Although an exact age is not known, the Buddha received his call quite early when he was about 19 years of age, renouncing his royal title and entering the life of a mendicant.

The Prophetess Avalokiteswara is considered much like the holy mother of Hindu and Christian tradition, although he/she was not the mother of the prophet, but rather a transcendental deific manifestation of the supreme Bodhisattva - the mother of compassion. (Avalokiteswara is perceived as being both male and female, in some images carrying characteristics of both sexes.)

"Mindful and fully aware the Bodhisattva passed away from the Heaven of the Contented and descended into his mother's womb."

"When the Bodhisattva had passed away from the Heaven of the Contented and entered his mother's womb, a great measureless light surpassing the splendour of the gods appeared in the world with its deities, its Maras and its Brahma divinities, in this generation with its monks and brahmans, with its princes and men. And even in those abysmal world interspaces of vacancy, gloom and utter darkness, where the moon and sun, powerful and mighty as they are, cannot make their light prevail - there too a great measureless light surpassing the splendour of the gods appeared; and the creatures born there perceived each other by that light: 'So it seems that other creatures have appeared here!' And this ten-thousandfold world-system shook and quaked and trembled; and there too a great measureless light surpassing the splendour of the gods appeared."

"When the Bodhisattva had descended into his mother's womb, four deities came to guard him from the four quarters, so that no human or non-human beings or anyone at all should harm him or his mother."

"When the Bodhisattva had descended into his mother's womb, she became intrinsically pure, refraining by necessity from killing living beings, from taking what is not given, from unchastity, from false speech, and from indulgence in wine, liquor and fermented brews."

"When the Bodhisattva had descended into his mother's womb, she at the same time possessed the five strands of sensual desires; and being endowed and furnished with them, she was gratified in them."

"When the Bodhisattva had descended into his mother's womb, no kind of affliction arose in her: she was blissful in the absence of all bodily fatigue. As though a blue, yellow, red, white, or brown thread were strung through a fine beryl gem of purest water, eight-faceted and well cut, so that a man with sound eyes, taking it in his hand, might review it thus 'This is a fine beryl gem of purest water, eight-faceted and well cut, and through it is strung a blue, yellow, red, white, or brown thread' - so too the Bodhisattva's mother saw him within her womb with all his limbs lacking no faculty."

"Seven days after the Bodhisattva was born, his mother died and was reborn in the Heaven of the Contented."

The Life of the Buddha, The Birth and the Early Years, Page 3-4, Translated by Bhikku Nanomoli, Buddhist Publication Society, 1972, (Buddhism, Words of the Buddha)

Auspicious Experience of the Prophet Buddha

"At that time in front of the Buddha a stupa of the seven precious things, five hundred yojanas in heights and two hundred and fifty yojanas in length and breadth, sprang up from the earth and abode in the sky. It was decorated with all kinds of precious things, splendidly adorned with five thousand parapets, thousands of myriads of recesses, and countless banners and flags; hung with jewel garlands, with myriads of kotis of gem bells suspended on it; on every side exhaling the fragrance of tamalapattra sandalwood, filling the whole world. All its streamers and canopies were composed of the precious seven, gold, silver, lapis lazuli, moonstone, agate, pearl, and carnelian, reaching up to the palaces of the four heavenly kings . . . Then from the midst of the Precious Stupa there came a loud voice, praising and saying: 'Excellent! Excellent! World-honored Sakyamuni! Thou art able to preach to the great assembly the Wonderful Law-Flower Sutra of universal and great wisdom, by which bodhisattvas are instructed and which the buddhas guard the mind . . . World Honored One! For what reason has this stupa sprung out of the earth and from its midst this voice proceeded?' Then the Buddha told the Bodhisattva Great Eloquence: 'In this stupa there is the whole body of the Tathagata. Of yore in the past innumerable thousand myriad kotis of asamkyeya worlds away in the east, there was a domain named Jewel Clear. In that [domain] there was a buddha entitled Abundant Treasures. When that buddha was treading the bodhisattva-way, he made a great vow, [saying]: 'After I become a buddha and am extinct, if in any country in the universe there be a place where the Law-Flower Sutra is preached, my stupa shall arise and appear there, in order that I may hearken to that sutra, bear testimony to it, and extol it, saying, 'Excellent!'"

The Threefold Lotus Sutra, The Lotus Sutra, Chapter XI, The Precious Stupa, Translated by Kato, Tamura and Miyasaka, Kosei Publishing, 1975 (Buddhism, Words of the Buddha)

Auspicious Death of the Prophet Buddha

"Soon after he had gone, Mara the Evil One came to the Blessed One and stood at one side. He said: 'Let the Blessed One attain final Nibbana now, let the Sublime One attain final Nibbana now. Now is the time for the Blessed One to attain final Nibbana. These words were once spoken by the Blessed One: 'I will not attain final Nibbana, Evil One, until the bhikkus, bhikkunis, laymen followers and laywoman followers, my disciples, are wise, disciplined, perfectly confident, and learned, until they remember the Dhamma (teachings) properly, practice the way of the Dhamma, practice the true way, and walk in the Dhamma, until after learning from their own teachers they announce and teach and declare and establish and reveal and expound and explain, until they can reasonably confute the theories of others that arise and can teach the Dhamma with its marvels.' But now all that has been accomplished. Let the Blessed One attain final Nibbana now. These words were spoken by the Blessed One: 'I will not attain final Nibbana, Evil One, until this holy life has become successful, prosperous, widespread, and disseminated among many, until it is well exemplified by men.' But now all that has been accomplished. Let the Blessed One attain final Nibbana now.'"

"When this was said, the Blessed One replied: 'You may rest, Evil One. Soon the Perfect One's attainment of final Nibbana will take place. Three months from now the Perfect One will attain final Nibbana.'"

"It was then, at the Capala Shrine, that the Blessed One, mindful and fully aware, relinquished the will to live. When he did so, there was a great earthquake, fearful and hair-raising, and the drums of heaven resounded. Knowing the meaning of this, the Blessed One then uttered this exclamation: 'The sage renounced the life-affirming will. Both measurable and immeasurable. And concentrated inwardly and

happy too, he shed his self-becoming . . ."
The Life of the Buddha, The Last Year, Page 303,
Translated by Bhikku Nanomoli, Buddhist
Publication Society, 1972, (Buddhism)

"Then the Blessed One addressed the bhikkus thus: 'Indeed, bhikkhus, I declare this to you: It is in the nature of all formations to dissolve. Attain perfection through diligence.' This was the Perfect One's last utterance."

"Then the Blessed One entered upon the first meditation. Emerging from that, he entered upon the second meditation. Emerging from that he entered upon the third meditation. Emerging from that he entered upon the fourth meditation. Emerging from that, he entered upon the base consisting of the infinity of space. Emerging from that, he entered upon the base consisting of the infinity of consciousness. Emerging from that, he entered upon the base consisting of nothingness. Emerging from that, he entered upon the base consisting of neither-perception-nor-non-perception. Emerging from that, he entered upon the cessation of perception and feeling."

" . . . Then the Blessed One, emerging from the cessation of perception and feeling, entered upon the base consisting of neither-perception-nor-non-perception. Emerging from that, he entered upon the base consisting of nothingness. Emerging from that, he entered upon the base consisting of the infinity of consciousness. Emerging from that, he entered upon the base consisting of the infinity of space. Emerging from that, he entered upon the fourth meditation. Emerging from that, he entered upon the third meditation. Emerging from that, he entered upon the second meditation. Emerging from that, he entered upon the first meditation. Emerging from that, he entered upon the second meditation. Emerging from that, he entered upon the third meditation. Emerging from that, he entered upon the fourth meditation. And on emerging from the fourth meditation, the Blessed One attained final Nibbana."

The Life of the Buddha, The Last Year, Page 324-325, Translated by Bhikku Nanomoli, Buddhist Publication Society, 1972, (Buddhism)

"With the Blessed One's attainment of final Nibbana, Sakka . . . uttered this stanza: 'Formations are impermanent, their very nature is to rise and fall. And there is none arises but must cease: True bliss lies in their stilling.'"

The Life of the Buddha, The Last Year, Page 325, Translated by Bhikku Nanomoli, Buddhist Publication Society, 1972, (Buddhism)

"My age is now full ripe, my life draws to its close: I leave you, I depart, relying on myself alone! Be earnest then, O brethren, holy, full of thought! Be steadfast in resolve! Keep watch o'er your own hearts! Who wearies not, but holds fast to his truth and law, shall cross this sea of life, shall make an end of grief."

The Teachings of the Compassionate Buddha, Book One, Part Seven, Mahaparinibbana Suttanta, Second Portion for Recitation, Compiled by E.A. Burtt, Mentor, 1955, (Buddhism, Words of the Buddha)

Death According to the Prophet Buddha

"From all the buddhas I saw
I gained some realization
And was shown this liberation
By a succession of means."

"From them I learned the inconceivable
Reality of liberation over countless eons,
Imbibing all at once the multitude of teachings
Projected by the buddhas when established therein."

"Those established therein
Go everywhere without attachment,
Instantly comprehending the countless
Names and groups of past, present, and future."

"They appear before all the multitudes
Of buddhas of all times,
Manifesting themselves in the presence
Of those buddhas as reflected images."

" . . . Then they ask the myriads of buddhas
Multitudes of questions
And remember the infinite teachings
Poured forth by the buddhas."

" . . . With bodies of infinite appearances,
They fill all realms, by the thousands;
They show an endless, endless variety of forms,

And all those forms in one."

"From each pore they emanate countless
Multitudes of light rays
And extinguish the fire of afflictions
Of all beings by various means."

"In this state, emanating myriad projected bodies
From each and every pore,
They pervade all realms with them
And guide beings with rain from the ocean of truth."

"This way of enlightenment, with inconceivable
forms,
Is the resort of all enlightening beings;
Based on this they carry out practices
In all lands for all time."

"Expounding the Teaching according to mentalities,
They remove the web of views;
Dwelling in ultimate felicity,
They show people the stage of omniscience."

"With inconceivably many bodies of endless forms
In all states of existence,
They teach according to mentality
Their forms reflections of all beings."

"So many and infinitely more,
As inconceivably many as atoms in all lands,
Are the oceans of manifestations of the fearless ones
When they have attained this peaceful liberation."

The Avatamsaka Sutra (The Flower Ornament Sutra),
Entry into the Realm of Reality, 1381-1383
Translated by Thomas Cleary, Shambhala, 1993
(Buddhism, Mahayana)

"The Master said to me: 'All the Buddhas and all sentient beings are nothing but universal mind, besides which nothing exists. This mind, which has always existed, is unborn and indestructive . . . If a man, when he is about to die, can only regard the five aggregates of his consciousness as voice, the four elements which compose his body as not constituting an ego, his true mind as formless and still, his true nature not as something which commenced at his birth and will perish at his death but as remaining utterly motionless, his mind and the objects of his perceptions as one - if he can only awake to this in a flash and remain free from the entanglements of the Triple World, he will indeed be one who leaves the world without the faintest tendency towards rebirth. If he should behold the lovely sight of all the Buddhas coming to welcome him, and yet feel no desire to go towards them; if he should behold all sorts of evil forms surrounding him and yet have no feeling of fear, but remain oblivious of self and at one with the Absolute, he will indeed achieve the formless state.'"

The Teachings of the Compassionate Buddha, Book Two, Part Five, Ultimate Reality Transcends What Can Be Expressed in Words, Hsi Yun, Compiled by E.A. Burtt, Mentor, 1955, (Buddhism, Words of the Buddha)

Auspicious Words of Confucius

Confucius
("Religions of the World," Page 231, The Granger Collection, By St. Martin's Press, 1993)

"The Master said, 'If out of the three hundred Songs I had to take one phrase to cover all my teaching, I would say 'Let there be no evil in your thoughts.'"

The Analects of Confucius, Book II, No. 2, Translated by Arthur Waley, Vintage Books, 1989, (Buddhism: Confucianism)

Auspicious Words of Lao Tzu

Lao Tzu
("Great Religions of the World," By the National Geographic Society, 1971)

"Act through nonaction,
Handle affairs through noninterference,
Taste what has no taste,
regard the small as great, the few as many,
Repay resentment with integrity.
Undertake difficult tasks
By approaching what is easy in them;
Do great deeds
By focusing on their minute aspects
All difficulties under heaven arise from what is easy.
All great things under heaven arise from what is minute."
Tao Te Ching, No. 26, Translated by Victor Mair,
Bantam Books, 1990, (Buddhism: Taoism)

Auspicious Words of Dogen

Dogen
("Moon in a Dewdrop," Edited by Kazuaki Tanahashi, Hokyo-Ji, Fukui
Prefecture, North Point Press, 1985)

"'Everyday mind' means to maintain an everyday mind in this world or in any world. Yesterday goes forth from this moment, and today comes forth from this place. With going the boundless sky goes, with coming the entire earth comes. This is everyday mind."

"Everyday mind opens the gate of the inner chamber. Because thousands of gates and myriads of doors open and close all at once, it is everyday mind. Now this boundless sky and entire earth are like unrecognized words, a voice from the deep. Words are all-inclusive, mind is all-inclusive, things are all-inclusive."

Moon in a Dewdrop, Body and Mind Study of the Way, No. 8, Edited by Kazuaki Tanahashi, North

Point Press, 1985, (Buddhism: Zen)

Auspicious Experiences of the Earth Store Bodhisattva

Earth Store Bodhisattva

("Sutra of the Past Vows of Earth Store Bodhisattva," Written by Same, Institute for the Advanced Studies of World Religions, Buddhist Text Translation Society, 1974)

"At that time the Four Heavenly Kings arose from their seats, put their palms together respectfully, and said to the Buddha, 'World-Honored One, since Earth Store Bodhisattva has made such extensive vows for kalpas, why then has he not yet completed his crossing over of beings? Why does he continue to practice such vast vows? Please, World Honored One, explain this for us.'"

"The Buddha told the Four Heavenly Kings, 'Excellent, excellent. For your benefit as well as for the benefit of men and gods of the present and future, I will speak of Earth Store Bodhisattva's works in the paths of birth and death . . . I shall speak of his expedient devices, and of his compassion and pity in rescuing, saving, crossing over, and liberating beings who are suffering for their offenses.'"

". . . From kalpas long ago until the present, Earth Store Bodhisattva has crossed over and liberated living beings, yet out of compassionate pity for those beings still suffering in the world, he has not yet completed his vows. Moreover, he sees that their causes for limitless kalpas in the future are like uncut tendrils and vines, and, because of this, he makes his mighty vows. Thus . . this Bodhisattva teaches and transforms beings by means of thousands of tens of thousands of myriads of expedient devices.'"

"Kings, to killers Earth Store Bodhisattva speaks of a retribution of a short lifespan; to robbers he speaks of a retribution of poverty and acute suffering; to practicers of sexual misconduct he speaks of the retribution of being born as pigeons, mandarin drakes and ducks; to the foul-mouthed he speaks of the retribution of a quarreling family."

"To slanderers he speaks of the retribution of tongue-less and cankerous mouth; to the hateful he speaks of being ugly and crippled; to the stingy he speaks of frustrated desires; to gluttons he speaks of the retribution of sickness, hunger, and thirst . . . "

Sutra of the Past Vows of Earth Store Bodhisattva,
Chapter Four, Page 130-131, Master Hsuan Hua,
Buddhist Text Translation Society, (Buddhism)

"Men and women in the future who do not practice good but do evil, who do not believe in cause and effect, who indulge in sexual misconduct and false speech, who practice double-tongued and harsh speech, and who slander the Great Vehicle, will certainly fall into Evil Paths. But if they encounter a good, knowing adviser who, in the flick of a finger, leads them to take refuge with Earth Store Bodhisattva, those living beings will obtain release from the retribution of the Three Evil Paths. Those whose acts show deference; who are respectful with a determined mind; who gaze in worship, praise, and make offerings of flowers, incense, clothing, gems, or food and drink will be born in the heavens. There they will enjoy supremely wonderful bliss for hundreds of thousands of kalpas."

Sutra of the Past Vows of Earth Store Bodhisattva, Chapter Four, Page 127, Master Hsuan Hua, Buddhist Text Translation Society, (Buddhism, Words of Earth Store Bodhisattva)

Auspicious Experience of Vimalakirti

Vimalakirti
("The Holy Teaching of Vimalakirti," Translated by Robert Thurman,
Cover, Pennsylvania State University Press, 1976)

"Thereupon the Lord touched the ground of this billion-world-galactic universe with his big toe, and suddenly it was transformed into a huge mass of precious jewels, a magnificent array of many hundreds of thousands of clusters of precious gems . . . Then, the Buddha said . . . " . . . do you see the splendor of the virtues of the buddha-field?'"

"When this splendor of the beauty of the virtues of the buddha-field shone forth, eighty-four thousand beings conceived the spirit of unexcelled perfect enlightenment."

" . . . Then, the Lord withdrew his miraculous power and at once the buddha-field was restored to its usual appearance."

The Holy Teaching of Vimalakirti, Chapter One, Page 18-19, Translated by Robert Thurman, Pennsylvania State University Press, 1990, (Buddhism)

Auspicious Experiences of Maitreya

Maitreya
("The Changeless Nature," By Arya Maitreya & Acarya Asanga,
Sherapalden Beru of Kagyu Samye Ling
- Artist, Karma Drubgyud Darjay Ling, 1979)

"One day, Maitripa saw light radiating from a crack in a stupa. He looked more closely and discovered those two texts. He read them but found them so profound that he doubted having understood their meaning absolutely clearly. He prayed earnestly to Maitreya, who appeared to him in a vision, gave him the verbal transmission of the text and inspired in him a confidence in its true meaning. Maitripa instructed many great scholars . . . "

The Changeless Nature, Introduction, No. 4, Page 6-7,
By Arya Matireya and Acarya Asanga, Karma
Drubgyud Darjay Ling, 1985, (Buddhism)

"Just as the gold fallen into the place arot with garbage was seen there by a god who then with great insistence showed the man that most supremely-beautiful of things, so that it might be completely cleansed, so also do the victors perceive that most precious, perfect buddhahood within all beings has fallen in the defilements' great mire and so they teach them all the dharma in order that it may be purified."

The Changeless Nature, Fourth Vajra Point, No. 111, By Arya Matreiya and Acarya Asanga, Karma Drubgyud Darjay Ling, 1985, (Buddhism)

Auspicious Experience of Milarepa

Milarepa

*("Tibet's Great Yogi, Milarepa" By W.Y. Evans-Wentz, From the book
'The Buddhism of Tibet,' By Dr. L.A. Waddell, Oxford University
Press, 1951)*

"At that time Retchung was in deep contemplation in his cell. For a whole night he had this dream: In an enchanting country called Ugyen (Abode of the Dakinis) he entered a great city where houses were built and tiled with precious material. The inhabitants of this city were of enchanting beauty, dressed in silk and adorned with ornaments of bone and precious stones. They did not speak, but only smiled joyfully and exchanged glances."

"Among them was a woman disciple of the Lama Tepuhwa, named Bharima, whom Retchung had known earlier in Nepal. She was dressed in red robes and seemed to be their leader. She said to Retchung, 'Nephew, you have come! Welcome.'

Having said this, she led him to a mansion made of precious stones and filled with a myriad of treasures to delight the senses. She treated him as an honored guest and set before him a great feast of food and drink."

"Then she said, 'At this moment, the Buddha Mikyupa, the immutable, is teaching the Doctrine at Ugyen. Nephew, if you wish to hear him I will ask his permission.'"

"Longing to hear him, Retchung answered, 'Yes, yes!' And they left together."

"At the center of the city, Retchung saw a great high throne of precious materials. Upon this throne sat the Buddha Immutable, resplendent and more sublime than he had visualized Him in meditation. He was teaching the Doctrine in the midst of an ocean of disciples. At this sign, drunk with joy, Retchung thought he would faint. Then Bharima said to him, 'Nephew, stay here for a moment. I will ask the Buddha's permission.'"

"She went forward and was granted her wish. Led by her, Retchung prostrated himself at the feet of the Buddha. He asked for a blessing and remained before him listening to the teaching."

The Buddha gazed at him for a moment with a smile, and Retchung thought to himself, 'He is thinking of me with compassion.' While listening to the history of the births and lives of the Buddhas and Bodhisattvas, the hairs on Retchung's body vibrated, and he believed."

Finally, the Buddha told the story of Tilopa, Naropa, and Marpa, which was even more astonishing than the preceding ones. And those who listened felt their faith grow."

"When he had finished, the Buddha said, 'Tomorrow I shall tell the story of Milarepa, a story still more wonderful than the ones I have just told. Let everyone come to hear it.'"

" . . . Feeling extraordinary veneration for the Master, he prayed to him from the depths of his heart and from the very marrow of his bones. While he was absorbed in a mixture of torpor and lucidity, he saw five beautiful young girls standing before him wearing the diadem and robes of Ugyen, one white, the others blue, yellow, red, and green. One of them said, 'The story of Milarepa will be told tomorrow, let us go and listen.'"

"A second said, 'Who will ask for it?' Another answered, 'The great spiritual sons will ask for it.' At the same time, their eyes were smiling at Retchung.

" . . . The young girl added, 'Everyone would be happy to hear such a marvelous teaching, so it is fitting that each of us ask for it with prayers . . .'"

"Then Retchung awoke from his trance . . . "

"Retchung prostrated himself and asked the Master about his health. Then, remaining on his knees and joining the palms of his hands, he addressed . . . prayer to the Master . . . tell us your story and your works . . . "

"Then, with smiling face, the Master answered, 'Because you ask, Retchung, I shall grant your prayer.'"

"The name of my clan is Khyungpo, my family name is Josay, and my name is Milarepa. In my youth

I committed black deeds. In maturity I practiced innocence. Now, released from both good and evil, I have destroyed the root of karmic action and shall have no reason for action in the future. To say more than this would only cause weeping and laughter. What good would it do to tell you? I am an old man. Leave me in peace.'"

" . . . Retchung prostrated himself and said . . . prayer . . . "

"Then the Venerable Master spoke as follows: 'Since you ask me with such pressing insistence, I will no longer hide my life from you, but will reveal it now."

The Life of Milarepa, Chapter One, Page 9-13,
Translated by Lobsang P. Lhalungpa, 1977,
(Buddhism)

Auspicious Experience of the 1st Dalai Lama, Gyalwa Gendun Druppa

"In the first watch of the night he performed the generation stage meditations of Highest Yoga Tantra . . . At midnight he slept for a short while, and then during the last watch of night he arose and engaged in meditation upon the completion stage yogas. Here he entered into the practice of the tantric method of breath meditation known as 'vajra recitation,' and by means of this technique established the absorption of the yoga of four voidnesses."

"Thus at dawn on the eighth day (half moon) of the twelfth month of the Wood Horse Year, when the master was in his eighty-fourth year, he manifested the external signs of dissolving into the four voidnesses, manifesting clear light realization and abiding in the state of Dharmakaya wisdom. Thus his attainment of perfection was made evident."

Training the Mind in the Great Way, Introduction, Page 33, Translated by Glenn Mullin, Snow Lion Publications, 1993, (Buddhism)

Auspicious Birth of the 14th Dalai Lama

The 14th Dalai Lama
("The Path to Enlightenment," By the 14th Dalai Lama, Cover, Snow Lion Publications, 1982)

"As soon as the child saw the Lama, he ran to him shouting 'Lama! Lama!,' despite the fact that the Rinpoche was in disguise and the word 'Lama' is 'Aga' in the Amdo dialect, which was the language of the area and which was always spoken in the boy's house. Seating himself in the Lama's lap, he grabbed a rosary which had belonged to the Great Thirteenth before it had been given to Keutsang Rinpoche. 'This is mine,' he said, 'please may I have it? . . . First, they presented him with both sets of rosaries, damarus, and walking-sticks, doggedly trying to conceal their excitement. The child did not hesitate over the rosaries or damarus, even though the 'wrong' damaru was much more brightly colored and more likely to appeal to a child. With the walking sticks, though, he appeared less certain. He held one, and then the other, but eventually he chose the right one. It was only later that the search party found that both walking sticks had belonged to the Thirteenth Dalai Lama . . . A physical examination revealed further signs traditionally associated with the Dalai Lama; a mark like a conch shell on the skin, for example, and two small bumps of flesh beneath the shoulder blades which represent the two extra arms with which Chenrezi is often shown."

Great Ocean, Chapter Two, Page 20-21, Hicks and Chogyan, Penguin, 1984, (Buddhism: Tibetan)

CHAPTER SIX
CHRISTIANITY

Jesus Christ

("Christ and the Fine Arts," The Ascension,' Gottlieb Peter Biermann - Artist, Page 469, Gramstorff Brothers, Inc., MA Harper & Row, 1938)

Mary

("Christ and the Fine Arts," 'The Sistine Madonna,' Raphael, Page 38, Harper & Row, 1938)

St. John the Baptist
*("The Bible in Art," Edited by Clifton Harby, Page 171, Titian -
Artist, 16th Century, Garden City Publishing Co., 1936)*

Auspicious Birth of the Prophet and Precursor, John the Baptist

The Prophet John the Baptist is said to have been born around 5 B.C. in Bethlehem to a humble family. John the Baptist received his call earlier than Jesus as he was the precursor, although an exact age for his call is not known.

"In the days of Herod, king of Judea, there was a priest named Zechariah of the priestly class of Abijah; his wife was a descendant of Aaron named Elizabeth. Both were just in the eyes of God, blamelessly following all the commandments and ordinances of the Lord. They were childless, for Elizabeth was sterile; moreover, both were advanced in years. Once, when it was the turn of Zechariah's class and he was fulfilling his functions as a priest before God, it fell to him by lot according to priestly usage to enter the sanctuary of the Lord and offer incense. While the full assembly of people was praying outside at the incense hour, an angel of the Lord appeared to him, standing at the right of the altar of incense. Zechariah was deeply disturbed upon seeing him, and overcome by fear. The angel said to him: 'Do not be frightened, Zechariah; your prayer has been heard. Your wife Elizabeth shall bear a son whom you shall name John. Joy and gladness will be yours, and many will rejoice at his birth; for he will be great in the eyes of the Lord. He will never drink wine or strong drink, and he will be filled with the Holy Spirit from his mother's womb. Many of the sons of Israel will he bring back to the Lord their God. God himself will go before him, in the spirit and power of Elijah, to turn the hearts of fathers to their children and the rebellious to the wisdom of the just, and to prepare for the Lord a people well-disposed.' Zechariah said to the angel: 'How am I to know this? I am an old man; my wife too is advanced in age.' The angel replied: 'I am Gabriel, who stand in attendance before God. I was sent to speak to you and bring you this good news. But now you will be mute - unable to speak - until the day these things take place, because you have not trusted my words. They will all come true in due season.' Meanwhile, the people were waiting for Zechariah, wondering at his delay in the temple. When he finally came out he was unable to speak to them and they realized that he had seen a vision inside. He kept making signs to them, for he remained speechless."

New American Bible, New Testament, Luke 1:5-24,
(Christianity)

"Here begins the gospel of Jesus Christ, the Son of God. In Isaiah the prophet it is written: 'I send my messenger before you to prepare your way: a herald's voice in the desert, crying, 'Make ready the way of the Lord, clear him a straight path.' Thus it was that John the Baptizer appeared in the desert, proclaiming a baptism of repentance which led to the forgiveness of sins."
New American Bible, New Testament, Mark 1:1-4,
(Christianity)

Auspicious Birth of the Messiah Jesus Christ

The Messiah Jesus Christ is said to have been born around 5 B.C. in Bethlehem to a poor family. Jesus Christ received his call to public ministry when he was 30 years of age.

"In the sixth month, the angel Gabriel was sent from God to a town of Galilee named Nazareth, to a virgin betrothed to a man named Joseph, of the house of David. The virgin's name was Mary. Upon arriving, the angel said to her: 'Rejoice, O highly favored daughter!' The Lord is with you. Blessed are you among women.' She was deeply troubled by his words, and wondered what his greeting meant. The angel went on to say to her: 'Do not fear, Mary You have found favor with God. You shall conceive and

bear a son and give him the name Jesus. Great will be
his dignity and he will be called Son of the Most
High. The Lord God will give him the throne of
David his father. He will rule over the house of Jacob
forever and his reign will be without end.' Mary said
to the angel, 'How can this be since I do not know
man?' The angel answered her: 'The Holy Spirit will
come upon you and the power of the Most High will
overshadow you; hence, the holy offspring to be born
will be called Son of God. Know that Elizabeth your
kinswoman has conceived a son in her old age; she
who was thought to be sterile is now in her sixth
month, for nothing is impossible with God.' Mary
said: 'I am the servant of the Lord. Let it be done to
me as you say.' With that the angel left her."
New American Bible, New Testament, Luke 1:26-38,
(Christianity)

"Now this is how the birth of Jesus Christ came
about. When his mother Mary was engaged to Joseph,
but before they lived together, she was found with
child through the power of the Holy Spirit. Joseph her
husband, an upright man unwilling to expose her to
the law, decided to divorce her quietly. Such was his
intention when suddenly the angel of the Lord
appeared in a dream and said to him: 'Joseph, son of
David, have no fear about taking Mary as your wife.
It is by the Holy Spirit that she has conceived this
child. She is to have a son and you are to name him
Jesus because he will save his people from their sins.'
All this happened to fulfill what the Lord had said
through the prophet: 'The virgin shall be with child

and give birth to a son, and they shall call him Emmanuel,' a name which means 'God is with us.' When Joseph awoke he did as the angel of the Lord had directed him and received her into his home as his wife."

New American Bible, New Testament, Matthew 1:18-25, (Christianity)

Auspicious Experience of the Prophet and Precursor, John the Baptist

"When John the Baptizer made his appearance as a preacher in the desert of Judea, this was his theme: 'Reform your lives! The Reign of God is at hand.' It was of him that the prophet Isaiah had spoken when he said: 'A herald's voice in the desert: Prepare the way of the Lord, make straight his paths.' John was clothed in a garment of camel's hair, and wore a leather belt around his waist. Grasshoppers and wild honey were his food. At that time Jerusalem, all Judea, and the whole region around the Jordan were going out to him. They were being baptized by him in the Jordan River as they confessed their sins . . . 'I baptize you in water for the sake of reform, but the one who will follow me is more powerful than I. I am not even fit to carry his sandals. He it is who will baptize you in the Holy Spirit and fire. His winnowing-fan is in his hand. He will clear the threshing floor and gather his grain into the barn, but the chaff he will burn in unquenchable fire.'"

"Later Jesus, coming from Galilee, appeared

before John at the Jordan to be baptized by him. John tried to refuse him with the protest, 'I should be baptized by you, yet you come to me!' Jesus answered: 'Give in for now. We must do this if we would fulfill all of God's demands.' So John gave in. After Jesus was baptized, he came directly out of the water. Suddenly the sky opened and he saw the Spirit of God descend like a dove and hover over him. With that, a voice from the heavens said, 'This is my beloved son. My favor rests on him.'"

New American Bible, New Testament, Matthew 3: 1-17, (Christianity)

"He went about the entire region of the Jordan proclaiming a baptism of repentance which led to the forgiveness of sins, as is written in the book of the words of Isaiah the prophet: 'A herald's voice in the desert, crying, 'Make ready the way of the Lord. Clear him a straight path. Every valley shall be filled and every mountain and hill shall be leveled. The windings shall be made straight and the rough ways smooth, and all mankind shall see the salvation of God.'"

" . . . When all the people were baptized, and Jesus was at prayer after likewise being baptized, the skies opened and the Holy Spirit descended on him in visible form like a dove. A voice from heaven was heard to say: 'You are my beloved Son. On you my favor rests.'"

New American Bible, New Testament, Luke 3:3-22, (Christianity)

Auspicious Experiences of the Messiah Jesus Christ

"Jesus said to all: 'Whoever wishes to be my follower must deny his very self, take up his cross each day, and follow in my steps. Whoever would save his life will lose it, and whoever loses his life for my sake will save it. What profit does he show who gains the whole world and destroys himself in the process? If a man is ashamed of me and my doctrine, the Son of Man will be ashamed of him when he comes in his glory and that of his Father and his holy angels. I assure you, there are some standing here who will not taste death until they see the reign of God.'"

"About eight days after saying this he took Peter, John and James, and went up onto a mountain to pray. While he was praying, his face changed in appearance and his clothes became dazzlingly white. Suddenly two men were talking with him - Moses and Elijah. They appeared in glory and spoke of his passage, which he was about to fulfill in Jerusalem. Peter and those with him had fallen into a deep sleep; but awakening, they saw his glory and likewise saw the two men who were standing with him. When these were leaving, Peter said to Jesus, 'Master, how good it is for us to be here. Let us set up three booths, one for you, one for Moses, and one for Elijah.' (He did not really know what he was saying.) While he was speaking, a cloud came and overshadowed them, and the disciples grew fearful as the others entered it. Then from the cloud came a voice which said, 'This is my Son, my Chosen One. Listen to him.' When the voice fell silent, Jesus was there alone. The disciples kept quiet, telling nothing of what they had seen at that time to anyone."

New American Bible, New Testament, Luke 9:23-36, (Christianity)

"Then Jesus was led into the desert by the Spirit to be tempted by the devil. He fasted forty days and forty nights, and afterward was hungry. The tempter approached and said to him, 'If you are the Son of God, command these stones to turn into bread.' Jesus replied, 'Scripture has it: 'Not on bread alone is man to live but on every utterance that comes from the mouth of God.'' Next the devil took him to the holy city, set him on the parapet of the temple, and said, 'If you are the Son of God throw yourself down. Scripture has it: 'He will bid his angels take care of you; with their hands they will support you that you may never stumble on a stone.'' Jesus answered him, 'Scripture also has it: 'You shall not put the Lord your God to the test.'' The devil then took him to a very high mountain and displayed before him all the kingdoms of the world in their magnificence, promising, 'All these will I bestow on you if you prostrate yourself in homage before me.' At this, Jesus said to him, 'Away with you, Satan! Scripture has it: 'You shall do homage to the Lord your God; him alone shall you adore.'' At that the devil left him, and angels came and waited on him."

New American Bible, New Testament, Matthew 4:1-11, (Christianity)

Auspicious Death of the Prophet and Precursor, John the Baptist

"Herod feared John, knowing him to be an upright and holy man, and kept him in custody. When he heard him speak he was very much disturbed; yet he felt the attraction of his words. Herodias had her chance one day when Herod held a birthday dinner for his court circle, military officers, and the leading men of Galilee. Herodias' own daughter came in at one point and performed a dance which delighted Herod and his guests. The king told the girl, 'Ask for anything you want and I will give it to you.' He went so far as to swear to her: 'I will grant you whatever you ask, even to half my kingdom!' She went out and said to her mother, 'What shall I ask for?' The mother answered, 'The head of John the Baptizer.' At that the girl hurried back to the king's presence and made her request: 'I want you to give me, at once, the head of John the Baptizer on a platter.' The king bitterly regretted the request; yet because of his oath and the presence of the guests, he did not want to refuse her. He promptly dispatched an executioner, ordering him to bring back the Baptizer's head. The man went and beheaded John in the prison. He brought in the head on a platter and gave it to the girl, and the girl gave it to her mother. Later, when the disciples heard about this, they came and carried his body away and laid it in a tomb."

New American Bible, New Testament, Mark 6:20-29,
(Christianity)

Auspicious Death of the Messiah Jesus Christ

"Two others who were criminals were led along with him to be crucified. When they came to Skull place, as it was called, they crucified him there and the criminals as well, one on his right and the other on his left. [Jesus said, 'Father, forgive them; they do not know what they are doing.'] They divided his garments, rolling dice for them. The people stood there watching and the leaders kept jeering at him, saying 'He saved others; let him save himself if he is the Messiah of God, the chosen one.' The soldiers also made fun of him, coming forward to offer him their sour wine and saying, 'If you are the king of the Jews, save yourself.' There was an inscription over his head: 'THIS IS THE KING OF THE JEWS.' One of the criminals hanging in crucifixion blasphemed him: Aren't you the Messiah? Then save yourself and us.' But the other one rebuked him: 'Have you no fear of God, seeing you are under the same sentence? We deserve it, after all. We are only paying the price for what we've done, but this man has done nothing wrong.' He then said, 'Jesus, remember me when you enter upon your reign.' And Jesus replied, 'I assure you: this day you will be with me in paradise.'"

"It was now around midday, and darkness came over the whole land until midafternoon with an eclipse of the sun. The curtain in the sanctuary was torn in two. Jesus uttered a loud cry and said, 'Father, into your hands I commend my spirit.' After he said this, he expired. The centurion, upon seeing what had happened gave glory to God by saying, 'Surely this was an innocent man.' When the crowd which had assembled for this spectacle saw what had happened, they went home beating their breasts."

New American Bible, New Testament, Luke 23:32-48, (Christianity)

Auspicious Resurrection of the Messiah Jesus Christ

"After the sabbath, as the first day of the week was dawning, Mary Magdalene came with the other Mary to inspect the tomb. Suddenly there was a mighty earthquake, as the angel of the Lord descended from heaven. He came to the stone, rolled it back, and sat on it. In appearance he resembled a flash of lightning while his garments were as dazzling as snow. The guards grew paralyzed with fear of him and fell down like dead men. Then the angel spoke, addressing the women: 'Do not be frightened. I know you are looking for Jesus the crucified, but he is not here. He has been raised, exactly as he promised. Come and see the place where he was laid. Then go quickly and tell his disciples: 'He has been raised from the dead and now goes ahead of you to Galilee, where you will see him.' That is the message I have for you.'"

New American Bible, New Testament, Matthew 28:1-7, (Christianity)

Death According to the Messiah Jesus Christ

'Try to come in through the narrow door. Many, I tell you, will try to enter and be unable. When once the master of the house has risen to lock the door and you stand outside knocking and saying, 'Sir, open for us,' he will say in reply, 'I do not know where you come from.' Then you will begin to say, 'We ate and drank in your company. You taught in our streets.' But he will answer, 'I tell you, I do not know where you come from. Away from me, you evildoers! There will be wailing and grinding of teeth when you see Abraham, Isaac, Jacob, and all the prophets safe in the kingdom of God, and you yourselves rejected. People will come from the east and the west, from the north and the south, and will take their place at the feast in the kingdom of God. Some who are last will be first and some who are first will be last.'"

New American Bible, New Testament, Luke 13:24-30,
(Christianity)

"His listeners asked him, 'Who, then, can be saved?' to which he replied, 'Things that are impossible for men are possible for God.'"

New American Bible, New Testament, Luke 18:26-27,
(Christianity)

"Then I saw new heavens and a new earth. The former heavens and the former earth had passed away, and the sea was no longer. I also saw a New Jerusalem, the holy city, coming down out of heaven

114

from God, beautiful as a bride prepared to meet her husband. I heard a loud voice from the throne cry out: 'This is God's dwelling among men. He shall dwell with them and they shall be his people and he shall be their God who is always with them. He shall wipe every tear from their eyes, and there shall be no more death or mourning, crying out or pain, for the former world has passed away.' The One who sat on the throne said to me, 'See, I make all things new!' Then he said, 'Write these matters down, for the words are trustworthy and true!' He went on to say: 'These words are already fulfilled! I am the Alpha and Omega, the Beginning and the End. To anyone who thirsts I will give to drink without cost from the spring of life-giving water. He who wins the victory shall inherit these gifts; I will be his God and he shall be my son. As for the cowards and traitors to the faith, the depraved and murderers, the fornicators and sorcerers, the idol-worshipers and deceivers of every sort - their lot is the fiery pool of burning sulphur, the second death!'"

New American Bible, New Testament, Revelations 21:1-8, (Christianity)

"Anyone who loves me will be true to my word, and my Father will love him; we will come to him and make our dwelling place with him. He who does not love me does not keep my words. Yet the word you hear is not mine; it comes from the Father who sent me . . . Peace is my farewell to you, my peace is my gift to you; I do not give it to you as the world gives peace."

New American Bible, New Testament, John 14:23-27, (Christianity)

"Jesus continued again in the discourse and said unto his disciples: 'When I shall have gone into the Light, then herald it unto the whole world and say unto them: Cease not to seek day and night and remit not yourselves until ye find the mysteries of the Light-Kingdom, which will purify you and make you into refined light and lead you into the Light-kingdom. 'Say unto them: Renounce the whole world and the whole matter therein and all its cares and all its sins, in a word all its associations which are in it, that ye may be worthy of the mysteries of the Light and be saved from all the chastisements which are in the judgments."

The Pistis Sophia, Third Book, Page 213, Translated by G.R.S. Mead, Spiritual Science Library, 1984, (Christianity: Gnostic, Words of Christ)

"And the Saviour answered and said unto Mary in the midst of his disciples: 'Amen, amen, I say unto you: All men who shall receive the mysteries of the Ineffable and moreover the mysteries of the First Mystery, sin every time through the compulsion of the Fate, and if they, when they are still in life, turn and repent and abide in any of their mysteries, it will be forgiven them at every time, because those mysteries are compassionate and forgiving for all time. For this cause then have I said unto you before: Those mysteries will not only forgive them their sins which they have committed from the beginning onwards, but they do not impute them to them from this hour onwards, - of which I have said unto you that they receive repentance at any time, and that they also will forgive the sins which they commit anew."

The Pistis Sophia, Third Book, Page 256, Translated by G.R.S. Mead, Spiritual Science Library, 1984, (Christianity: Gnostic, Words of Christ)

Auspicious Experiences of St. Peter

Peter
*("The Bible in Art," By Clifton Harby, Il Perugino - Artist, Page 381,
Sistine Chapel, Garden City Publishing Co., 1936)*

"Uriel (Urael) the angel of God shall bring forth the souls of those sinners (every one according to his transgression . . .) . . . Then shall men and women come unto the place prepared for them. By their tongues wherewith they have blasphemed the way of righteousness shall they be hanged up. There is spread under them unquenchable fire, that they escape it not. Behold, another place: therein is a pit, great and full (of . . .) In it are they that have denied righteousness: and angels of punishment chastise them and there do they kindle upon them the fire of their torment."

"And again behold [two: corrupt] women: they hang them up by their neck and by their hair; they shall cast them into the pit. These are they which plaited their hair, not for good (or, not to make them beautiful) but to turn them to fornication, that they might ensnare the souls of men unto perdition. And the men that lay with them in fornication shall be hung by their loins in that place of fire; and they shall say one to another: We knew not that we should come into everlasting punishment."

And the murderers and them that have made common cause with them shall they cast into the fire, in a place full of venomous beasts, and they shall be tormented without rest, feeling their pains; and their worms shall be as many in number as a dark cloud . . . And the angel Ezrael shall bring forth the souls of them that have been slain, and they shall behold the torment of them that slew them, and say one to another: Righteousness and justice is the judgement of God. For we heard, but we believed not, that we should come into this place of eternal judgment."

"And near by this flame shall be a pit, great and very deep, and into it floweth from above all manner of torment, foulness and issue . . . "

"And my Lord Jesus Christ our king said unto me: Let us go unto the holy mountain. And his disciples went with him, praying. And behold there were two men there, and we could not look upon their faces, for a light came from them, shining more than the sun, and their raiment also was shining, and cannot be described, and nothing is sufficient to be compared unto them in this world. And the sweetness of them . . . that no mouth is able to utter the beauty of their appearance for their aspect was astonishing and wonderful. And the other, great, I say, (probably: and, in a word, I cannot describe it), shineth in his aspect above crystal. Like the flower of roses is the appearance of the colour of his aspect and of his body . . . his head (al. their head was a marvel). And upon his (their) shoulders . . . and on their foreheads was a crown of nard woven of fair flowers. As the rainbow in the water, so was their hair. And such was the comeliness of their countenance, adorned with all manner of ornament. And when we saw them on a sudden, we marveled. And I drew near unto the Lord (God) Jesus Christ and said unto him: O my Lord, who are these? And he said unto him: Abraham and Isaac and Jacob and the rest of the righteous fathers? And he showed us a great garden, open, full of fair trees and blessed fruits, and the odour of perfumes. The fragrance thereof was pleasant and came even unto us. And thereof . . . saw I much fruit. And my Lord and God Jesus Christ said unto me: Hast thou seen the companies of the fathers?"

"As is their rest, such also is the honour and the glory of them that are persecuted for my righteousness sake. And I rejoiced and believed and understood that which is written in the book of my Lord Jesus Christ . . . "

"Peter opened his mouth and said to me: Hearken, my son Clement . . . "The Son at his coming will raise the dead . . . and will make my righteous ones shine seven times more than the sun, and will make their crowns shine like crystal and like the rainbow in the time of rain, (crowns) which are perfumed with nard and cannot be contemplated, (adorned) with rubies, with the colour of emeralds shining brightly, with topazes, gems, and yellow pearls that shine like the stars of heaven, and like the rays of the sun, sparkling which cannot be gazed upon.' Again, of the angels: 'Their faces shine more than the sun; their crowns are as the rainbow in the time of rain. (They are perfumed) with nard. Their eyes shine like the morning star. The beauty of their appearance cannot be expressed . . . Their raiment is not woven, but white as that of the fuller . . . And being afraid we forgat all the things of this life and of the flesh, and knew not what we said because of the greatness of the wonder of that day, and of the mountain whereon he showed us the second coming in the kingdom that passeth not away."

The Apocryphal New Testament, Apocalypse of Paul, Page 518-520, Translated by Montague Rhodes James, Oxford, 1924, (Christianity)

"And then shall all men pass through a blazing river and unquenchable flame, and the righteous shall be saved whole, all of them, but the ungodly shall perish therein unto all ages."

The Apocryphal New Testament, Second Book of the Sibylline Oracles, Page 523, Translated by Montague Rhodes James, Oxford, 1924, (Christianity)

The Apocalypses of Peter and Paul are well detailed accounts of visions of heaven and hell received by Peter and Paul after the resurrection of Christ from the hand of Christ. The part of the text which kept 'The Apocalypse of Peter' out of the New Testament is this one, which explains that hell is not an eternal punishment, but rather, a punishment for a very long time . . . until?

"Next: 'The Father hath committed all judgement unto the Son' The destiny of sinners - their eternal doom - is more than Peter can endure: he appeals to Christ to have pity on them."

"And my Lord answered me and said to me: 'Hast thou understood that which I said unto thee before? It is permitted unto thee to know that concerning which thou askest: but thou must not tell that which thou hearest unto the sinners lest they transgress the more, and sin.' Peter weeps many hours, and is at last consoled by an answer which, though exceedingly diffuse and vague, does seem to promise ultimate pardon for all: 'My Father will give unto them all the life, the glory, and the kingdom that passeth not away,' . . . 'It is because of them that have believed in me that I am come. It is also because of them that have believed in me, that, at their word, I shall have pity on men.' The doctrine that sinners will be saved at last by the prayers of the righteous, is rather obscurely, enunciated in the Second Book of the Sibylline Oracles (a paraphrase, in this part, of the Apocalypse), and in the (Coptic) Apocalypse of Elias."

"Ultimately Peter orders Clement to hide this revelation in a box, that foolish men may not see it."

" . . . The passage in the Coptic Apocalypse of Elias is guarded and obscure in expression, but significant. It begins with a sentence which has a parallel in Peter."

"The righteous will behold the sinners in their punishment, and those who have persecuted them and delivered them up. Then will the sinners on their part behold the place of the righteous and be

partakers of grace. In that day will that for which the (righteous) shall often pray, be granted to them."
The Apocryphal New Testament, Apocalypse of Peter, Page 518-521, Translated by Montague Rhodes James, Oxford, 1924, (Christianity)

Auspicious Experience of St. Paul

St. Paul
("The Book of Life," By Newton Marshall and Irving Francis Wood,
Volume 7, Page 1, Raphael Sanzio - Artist, Vatican Gallery, John
Rudin & Co. Inc., 1923)

" . . . And the angel answered and said unto me: Follow me, and I will show thee the place of the righteous where they are taken when they are dead."

"And I went after the angel, and he took me into heaven, and I looked upon the firmament, and saw there the powers; and there was forgetfulness which deceiveth and draweth unto itself the hearts of men, and the spirit of slander and the spirit of fornication and the spirit of wrath and the spirit of insolence, and there were the princes of wickedness. These things saw I beneath the firmament of the heaven."

"And again I looked and saw angels without mercy, having no pity, whose countenances were full of fury, and their teeth sticking forth out of their mouth: their eyes shone like the morning star of the east, and out of the hairs of and out of their mouth went forth sparks of fire. And I asked the angel, saying: Who are these, Lord? And the angel answered and said unto me: These are they which are appointed unto the souls of sinners in the hour of necessity, even of them that have not believed that they had the Lord for their helper and have not trusted in him."

"And I looked into the height and beheld other angels whose faces shone like the sun, and their loins were girt with golden girdles, holding palms in their hands, and the sign of God, clad in raiment whereon was written the name of the Son of God, full of all gentleness and mercy. And I asked the angel and said: Who are these, Lord, that are of so great beauty and compassion? And the angel answered and said unto me: These are the angels of righteousness that are sent to bring the souls of the righteous in the hour of necessity, even them that have believed that they had the Lord for their helper. And I said unto him: Do the righteous and the sinners of necessity meet (witnesses) when they are dead? And the angel answered and said unto me: The way whereby all pass unto God is one: but the righteous having an holy helper with them are not troubled when they go to appear in the presence of God."

"And I said unto the angel: I would see the souls of the righteous and of the sinners as they depart out of the world. And the angel answered and said unto me: Look down upon the earth. And I looked down from heaven upon the earth and beheld the whole world, and it was as nothing in my sight; and I saw the children of men as though they were naught, and failing utterly; and I marveled, and said unto the angel: Is this the greatness of men? And the angel answered and said unto me: This it is . . ."

The Apocryphal New Testament, Apocalypse of Paul, Page 529-530, Translated by Montague Rhodes James, Oxford, 1924, (Christianity)

Auspicious Finding of the Apocalypse of St. Paul

"At what time was it made manifest? In the consulate of Theodosius Augustus the younger and Cynegius, a certain honourable then dwelling at Tarsus, in the house which had been the house of Saint Paul, an angel appeared unto him by night and gave him a revelation, saying that he should break up the foundation of the house and publish that which he found; but he thought this to be a lying vision. But a third time the angel came, and scourged him and compelled him to break up the foundation. And he dug, and found a box of marble inscribed upon the sides: therein was the revelation of Saint Paul, and his shoes wherein he walked when he taught the word of God. But he feared to open that box, and brought it to the judge: and the judge took it, sealed as it was with lead, and sent it to the emperor Theodosius, fearing that it might be somewhat strange; and the emperor when he received it, opened it and found the revelation of St. Paul. A copy thereof he sent to Jerusalem and the original he kept with him."

The Apocryphal New Testament, Apocalypse of Paul, Page 526, Translated by Montague Rhodes James,

Oxford, 1924, (Christianity)

Auspicious Experience of St. Francis of Assisi

St. Francis of Assisi
("The Francis Book," Compiled by Roy M. Gasnick, Page 129,
Ludovico Dardi da Cigoli - Artist, MacMillan Publishers, 1980)

"And when he came to the place where St. Francis was praying, he stopped at a certain distance, for he began to hear a number of persons talking. Going nearer in order to see and hear more clearly what they were saying, he perceived a marvelous light completely surrounding St. Francis, and in that light he saw Christ and the Blessed Virgin and St. John the Baptist and St. John the Evangelist and a great throng of angels, who were talking with St. Francis."

The Little Flowers of St. Francis, Part One, No. 17,
Translated by Raphael Brown, Doubleday Image,
1958, (Christianity)

"The next day came, that is, the Feast of the Cross. And St. Francis, sometime before dawn, began to pray outside the entrance of his cell . . . : 'My Lord Jesus Christ, I pray You to grant me two graces before I die: the first is that during my life I may feel in my soul and in my body, as much as possible, that pain which You, dear Jesus, sustained in the hour of Your most bitter Passion. The second is that I may feel in my heart, as much as possible, that excessive love with which You, O Son of God, were inflamed in willingly enduring such suffering for us sinners.'"

" . . . And the fervor of his devotion increased so much within him that he utterly transformed himself into Jesus through love and compassion. And while he was thus inflaming himself in this contemplation, on that same morning he saw coming down from Heaven a Seraph with six resplendent and flaming wings. As the Seraph, flying swiftly, came closer to St. Francis, so that he could perceive Him clearly, he noticed that He had the likeness of a Crucified Man, and His wings were so disposed that two wings extended above His head, two were spread out to fly, and the other two covered His entire body."

" . . . During this marvelous apparition, all of Mount Alverna seemed to be on fire with very bright flames, which shone in the night and illumined the various surrounding mountains and valleys more clearly than if the sun were shining over the earth."

"Now when, after a long time and a secret conversation, this wonderful vision disappeared . . . it left a marvelous image and imprint of the Passion of Christ in his flesh. For soon there began to appear in the hands and feet of St. Francis the marks of nails such as he had just seen in the body of Jesus Crucified, who had appeared to him in the form of a Seraph."

The Little Flowers of St. Francis, Part Two, Third Consideration, Page 190-192, Translated by Raphael Brown, Doubleday Image, 1958, (Christianity)

Auspicious Experience of St. Catherine of Siena

St. Catherine of Siena

("Mysteries, Marvels and Miracles in the Lives of the Saints," Page 42,
By Joan Carroll Cruz, From the Book 'The Life of Catherine of Siena,
By Blessed Raymond of Capua, TAN Books, 1997)

"While they were on the way back from their sister's house to their own and were passing along a certain valley, called by the people Valle Piatta, the holy child, lifting her eyes, saw on the opposite side above the Church of the Preaching Friars a most beautiful room, adorned with regal magnificence, in which was seated, on an imperial throne, Jesus Christ, the Saviour of the world, clothed in pontifical vestments, and wearing on His head a papal tiara; with Him were the princes of the Apostles, Peter and Paul, and the holy evangelist John. Astounded at such a sight, Catherine stood still, and with fixed and immovable look, gazed, full of love, on her Saviour, who, appearing in so marvellous a manner, in order sweetly to gain her love to Himself, fixed on her the eyes of His Majesty, and, with a tender smile, lifted over her His right hand, and, making the sign of the Holy Cross in the manner of a bishop, left with her the gift of His eternal benediction . . . "

"The Dialogues of St. Catherine of Siena was dictated to her secretaries by the Saint in ecstasy."

The Dialogue of St. Catherine of Siena, Introduction, Page 12-13, 22, Translated by Algar Thorold, Tan Books, 1974, (Christianity: Catholic)

Auspicious Experience of St. Teresa of Avila

St. Teresa of Avila
("Mysteries, Marvels and Miracles in the Lives of the Saints," Page 46,
By Joan Carroll Cruz, TAN Books, 1997)

"I was at prayer one day when suddenly, without knowing how, I found myself, as I thought, plunged right into hell. I realized that it was the Lord's will that I should see the place which the devils had prepared for me there and which I had merited for my sins. This happened in the briefest space of time, but, even if I were to live for many years, I believe it would be impossible for me to forget it. The entrance, I thought, resembled a very long, narrow passage, like a furnace, very low, dark and closely confined; the ground seemed to be full of water which looked like filthy, evil-smelling mud, and in it were many wicked-looking reptiles. At the end there was a hollow place scooped out of a wall, like a cupboard, and it was here that I found myself in close confinement. But the sight of all this was pleasant by comparison with what I felt there. What I have said is in no way an exaggeration."

" . . . In that pestilential spot, where I was quite powerless to hope for comfort, it was impossible to sit or lie, for there was no room to do so. I had been put in this place which looked like a hole in the wall, and those very walls, so terrible to the sight, bore down upon me and completely stifled me. There was no light and everything was in the blackest darkness. I do not understand how this can be, but, although there was no light, it was possible to see everything the sight of which can cause affliction. At that time it was not the Lord's will that I should see more of hell itself, but I have since seen another vision of frightful things, which are the punishment of certain vices."

"I repeat, then, that this vision was one of the most signal favours which the Lord has bestowed upon me: it has been of the greatest benefit to me, both in taking from all the fear of the tribulations and disappointments of this life and also in strengthening me to suffer them and to give thanks to the Lord, Who, as I now believe, has delivered me from such terrible and never-ending torments."

The Life of Teresa of Jesus, Chapter XXXII, Page 301-302, Translated by E. Allison Peers, Image Doubleday, 1960, (Christianity: Catholic)

Auspicious Experience of St. John of the Cross

St. John of the Cross
*("Mysteries, Marvels and Miracles in the Lives of the Saints," Page 47,
By Joan Carroll Cruz, TAN Books, 1997)*

"One day St. John of the Cross handed Ana Maria de Jesus, a holy nun at the Incarnation, a small piece of paper on which he had drawn in pen and ink a picture of Christ on the cross. It represented a vision he had recently had. Fortunately the small drawing has not been lost, but is still preserved in a reliquary at the Convent of the Incarnation in Avila. This is an enlarged photo of the original."
The Collected Works of St. John of the Cross, Note on Drawing of Christ on the Cross, Page 39, Translated by Kavanaugh and Rodroguez, ICS Publications, 1979, (Christianity: Catholic)

CHRIST CRUCIFIED
A DRAWING BY ST. JOHN OF THE CROSS

St. John of the Cross's Drawing of his Vision
*The Collected Works of St. John of the Cross, Note on Drawing
of Christ on the Cross, Page 39, Translated by Kavanaugh and
Rodroguez, ICS Publications, 1979, (Christianity: Catholic)*

Auspicious Experiences of Mary of Agreda, Anne Catherine Emmerich and Maria Valtora

Venerable Mary of Agreda
*("A Popular Abridgement of 'The Mystical City of God,'" By
Venerable Mary of Agreda, Cover, TAN Books, 1978)*

Ven. Anne Catherine Emmerich
*("The Life of Christ and Biblical Revelations," By Ven. Anne Catherine
Emmerich, TAN Books, 1986)*

Mary of Agreda and Anne Catherine Emmerich were two of the most well-known of several saints who received extensive visions of the life and death of Jesus Christ, the Blessed Virgin Mary and other Biblical events. Mary of Agreda wrote a four-volume work entitled 'The Mystical City of God' about the life of the Blessed Virgin Mary while Anne Catherine Emmerich wrote a four-volume work entitled 'The Life of Jesus Christ and Biblical Revelations,' being the inspiration and basis for the movie 'The Passion of the Christ,' produced by Mel Gibson in 2003. Maria Valtorta is a recent addition to this list of auspicious mystics, who lived from 1897 - 1961 in Italy. Her tremendous addition to this body of literature is 'The Poem of the Man-God,' a five-volume work on the Life and Death of Jesus Christ.

One of the unique features of Mary of Agreda and Maria Valtorta's works is that each chapter contains an instruction from the Blessed Virgin Mary or Jesus Christ Himself (in their words) to the reader on attaining unto a holy state of life.

Another interesting feature of Anne Catherine Emmerich and Maria Valtorta's lives were the fact that both were bedridden for nearly thirty years. It was in this auspicious circumstance that each of these two mystics were able to remain in the space required for them to receive such profound visitations from the Lord.

Emanuel Swedenborg
(Swedenborg Foundation)

"May they know, then, that every child, wherever he was born - within the church or outside it, of godly or godless parents - every child is accepted by the Lord when he dies and is brought up to heaven. According to Divine design, he is taught and filled with insights into what is true. Then, as he is made complete in understanding and wisdom, he is introduced into heaven and becomes an angel."

Heaven and Hell, Chapter 37, No. 329, Translated by George Dole, Swedenborg Foundation, 1976, (Christianity)

"Since there is infinite diversity in heaven - no one community or even angel is quite like another - heaven is divided overall, regionally, and locally. Overall, it is divided into two kingdoms, regionally into three heavens, and locally into countless communities."

Heaven and Hell, Chapter 4, No. 20, Translated by George Dole, Swedenborg Foundation, 1976, (Christianity)

Auspicious Experience of Hildegard of Bingen

Hildegard Von Bingen
("Book of Divine Works," By Hildegard Von Bingen, Page ii, Angela
Werneke - Artist, Bear & Co., 1987)

"A great band of angels lives mysteriously with God in heaven. With their light they radiate through the Godhead even as they themselves remain hidden from human beings unless recognized by luminous signs. Because of its spiritual nature this band is more closely associated with God than with human beings. It appears only rarely to men or women. In contrast, other angels, who are in contact with human beings, show themselves to us under certain forms in accord with God's will. Because God has prepared the angels for various offices, God has also decided that they should have the necessary contact with us. However varied may be the tasks they carry out, all of the angels revere the one God in devotion and knowledge."

Book of Divine Works, Third Part, Sixth Vision, 5,
Edited by Matthew Fox, Bear & Co., 1987,
(Christianity)

Auspicious Words of St. Alphonsus Liguori

St. Alphonsus Liguori
("The Great Means of Salvation and of Perfection," By St. Alphonsus Liguori, Cover, Redemptorist Fathers, 1927)

"If you purchase a house, you spare no pains to obtain all the securities necessary to guard against the loss of your money; if you take medicine, you are careful to assure yourself that it cannot injure you; if you pass over a torrent, you cautiously avoid all danger of falling into it; and for a miserable gratification, for a beastly pleasure, you will risk your eternal salvation."

Preparation for Death, Consideration XVIII, Third Point, Edited By Rev. Eugene Grimm, Redemptorist Fathers, 1926, (Christianity: Catholic)

Auspicious Experience and Death of St. Thomas Aquinas

St. Thomas Aquinas
*("Religions of the World," Page 383, The Granger Collection, Giovanni
Da Fiesole - Artist, St. Martin's Press, 1993)*

"The writing career of Thomas came suddenly to an end on December 6, 1273. While saying mass that morning a great change came over him, and afterwards he ceased to write or dictate. Urged by his companion to complete the Summa, he replied: 'I can do no more; such things have been revealed to me that all I have written seems as straw, and I now await the end of my life.' . . . Overcome by illness shortly after his departure from Naples, he retired to the Cistercian monastery of Fossanova. There he commented on the Song of Solomon at the request of the monks, and died, March 7, 1274."

Great Books of the Western World, Volume 19, Biographical Note, Page vi, Edited by Mortimer

Adler, William Benton Publisher, Encyclopedia Britannica, 1952, (Compilation)

Auspicious Words of St. Therese of Lisieux

St. Therese of Lisieux
*("Story of a Soul, Autobiography of St. Therese of Lisieux," Translated
by John Clarke, ICS Publications, 1975)*

"Striking deeds are forbidden me. I cannot preach the Gospel; I cannot shed my blood, but what matter? My brothers do it for me, while I, *a little child,* stay close beside the royal throne and *love* for those who are fighting."
The Story of a Soul, Chapter Eleven, Immense Desires, Page 202, Translated by Michael Day, Tan Publishers, 1951, (Christianity: Catholic)

Auspicious Experience of St. Padre Pio

Padre Pio
("The Agony of Jesus," By Padre Pio, Cover, Photograph Copyright Owner, Federico Abresch of San Giovanni Rotondu, Italy, TAN Books, 1974)

"Within the Mass, however, Padre Pio admitted to an intense mystical involvement with the unseen world. He apparently saw, as in a vision, the entire Passion, and actually felt, physically, the wounds of Jesus. When he read the Epistle and Gospel of the day's Mass, he identified so closely with their content that he frequently would shed copious tears. During the offering of the bread and wine, Padre Pio often remained motionless for moments on end, as if 'nailed by a mysterious force,' gazing with moistened eyes upon the crucifix. At these moments, he said, his soul was 'separated from all that is profane.' At the commemorations of the Living and the Dead, he maintained that he saw all his spiritual children at the altar, 'as if in a mirror.'"

"During the consecration, Padre Pio seemed to suffer most intensely. He seemed to feel the horrible weight of sin - his own sins and those of all mankind - and the enormity of God's immense and unmerited love. As he communed, he professed to feel physically the 'kiss of Jesus,' all over his being. He spoke of Communion as 'all one mercy, all one embrace . . . "

Padre Pio: The True Story, Chapter XXI, Page 242, By C. Bernard Ruffin, Our Sunday Visitor, 1982, (Christianity: Catholic)

Auspicious Stigmatization of St. Padre Pio

"All of a sudden, a great light shone round about my eyes. In the midst of this light there appeared the wounded Christ. He said nothing to me before He disappeared . . .' The crucifix in the choir, he said, transformed itself into a being: 'From Him there came forth beams of light with shafts of flame that wounded me in the hands and feet. My side had already been wounded on the fifth of August of the same year.' According to all accounts, when the ecstasy ended, Pio found his hands and feet perforated and bleeding. He lay on the floor, his side issuing great quantities of blood."

Padre Pio: The True Story, Chapter XI, The Stigmata, Page 140, By C. Bernard Ruffin, Our Sunday Visitor, 1982, (Christianity: Catholic)

Auspicious Words of St. Mother Teresa of Calcutta

Mother Teresa
("A Simple Path," Compiled by Lucinda Vardey, Cover, Ballantine Books, 1995)

"Holiness is not a luxury for the few; it is not just for some people. It is meant for you and for me, for all of us. It is a simple duty, because if we learn to love, we learn to be holy."

Loving Jesus, Chapter One, Page 4, Mother Teresa, Servant Publications, 1991, (Christianity)

CHAPTER SEVEN
NATIVE AMERICAN
(Tribal)

Short Bull, Lakota Holy Man (who was the Apostle of the 1890
Ghost Dance Preceding Wounded Knee)
*("The Encyclopedia of Native American Religion," By Arlene
Hirschfelder and Paulette Molin, Page 264, Photograph from the
National Anthropolical Archives, Smithsonian Institute, MJF Books,
1992)*

White Buffalo Calf Woman
(Famous Painting, Artist Unknown)

Auspicious Birth of Short Bull the Prophet

Among Native American and Tribal Religions, there are innumerable prophets and seers, most of which are given fairly equal footing with the other in those religions. Each of those religions holds different world views and perceptions of life and death. We have chosen one of those many, who emerged during a very auspicious time; the Ghost Dance Religion and the Battle of Wounded Knee. (Native American Lakota Sioux.) Tribal religions expand into hundreds of religious systems as you go from Native American to Hawaiian, Australian Aboriginal, African and the many other tribal cultures around the world.

The Prophet Short Bull is said to have been born in the mid 1800's amongst Chief Lip's band of Lakota Sioux located at Pass Creek between Rosebud and Pine Ridge in Dakota Territory. His call came after he had been a warrior, fighting in the Battle of the Little Big Horn and other intertribal wars. He received his call in 1889, although we do not know his age at that time.

White Buffalo Calf Woman was a prophetess or 'wakan' of many Native American tribes, bringing the gift of the Sacred Pipe to the people. Revered as a 'Holy Mother' she is held with great reverence by the Native people of the Americas.

Auspicious Experience of the Short Bull the Prophet

"Now, there will be a tree sprout up, and there all the members of our religion and the tribe must gather together. That will be the place where we will see our dead relations. But before this time we must dance the balance of this moon, at the end of which time the earth will shiver very hard. Whenever this thing occurs, I will start the wind to blow. We are the ones who will then see our fathers, mothers, and everybody. We, the tribe of Indians, are the ones who are living a sacred life. God, our father himself, has told and commanded and shown me to do these things."

"Our father in heaven has placed a mark eat each point of the four winds. First, a clay pipe, which lies at the setting of the sun and represents the Sioux tribe. Second, there is a holy arrow lying at the north, which represents the Cheyenne tribe. Third, at the rising of the sun there lies hail, representing the Arapaho tribe. Fourth, there lies a pipe and nice feather at the south, which represents the Crow tribe. My father has shown me these things, therefore we must continue this dance. If the soldiers surround you four deep, three of you, on whom I have put holy shirts, will sing a song, which I have taught you . . . "

The Ghost-Dance Religion and Wounded Knee, Chapter Ten, Short Bull's Sermon, By James Mooney, Dover, (Original Publication) 1896, (Tribal: Ghost Dance Religion, Oglala Sioux)

Auspicious Experience of White Buffalo Calf Woman the Prophetess

"According to belief, White Buffalo Calf Woman first appeared to two young men who were out hunting. As they stopped to scan the area for game, they saw someone approaching in the distance. When the mysterious person drew nearer, they saw a woman of great beauty clothed in white buckskin. One of the young men expressed bad thoughts toward her, but his companion warned him that she was most likely wakan, or sacred. When the mysterious woman reached the hunters, she called to the one with evil intentions. After approaching her, they were both enveloped by a cloud. When it lifted, all that remained of the man were his bones and the snakes that had eaten him. The mysterious woman then told the other hunter to return home and tell his chief, named Standing Hollow Horn in the account given by BLACK ELK, to prepare for her arrival. Upon reaching the camp, the young man related all that had happened. As instructed, a large tipi was built, and the people gathered together. They then waited for the mysterious person to arrive. Soon some of the people saw the holy woman approaching in the distance. After entering the tipi, she walked in a sunrise (clockwise) direction then stopped before the leader. The holy woman took a bundle from her back, removing a pipe and a round stone."

"She then gave the people sacred teachings. Beginning with the pipe, she explained its meaning and each of its components. She told the people that the pipestone bowl represented the earth, that the wood stem represented all of the earth's growing things, that a buffalo calf carved on the bowl represented all four-legged creatures and that the pipe's 12 feathers, from the spotted eagle, represented all winged creatures. Whoever prayed with it would be joined to all other life in the universe. The holy woman also instructed the people about the stone, explaining that the seven circles on it stood for the seven sacred rites. She presented the first rite, stating that the other six would be revealed in time and that the sacred pipe was to be used in each of them."

"After teaching the GHOST-KEEPING CEREMONY, the first rite, the holy woman walked in a sunwise (clockwise) direction around the tipi, then left. While walking away, she stopped and sat down. When she stood up, the people saw that she had been transformed into a red and brown buffalo calf. The calf continued on, stopped, lay down and arose as a white buffalo. The white buffalo repeated the same actions, becoming a black buffalo. This buffalo bowed to each quarter of the universe and then vanished from view."

The Encyclopedia of Native American Religion,
White Buffalo Calf Woman, Hirschfelder and Molin,
MJF Books, 1992, (Tribal: Native American, Oglala
Sioux)

Auspicious Death of Short Bull the Prophet

Before his death in 1924, Short Bull told those who asked that the Ghost Dance Religion (despite the tremendous tragedy which had come about at the massacre of Wounded Knee) had been a religion of peace.

Death According to the Ghost Dance Religion

"When we went to the place a smoke descended from heaven to the place where he was to come. When the smoke disappeared, there was a man of about forty, which was the Son of God. The man said:"

"'My grandchildren! I am glad you have come far away to see your relatives. This are your people who have come back from your country. 'When he said he want us to go with him, we looked and we saw a land created across the ocean on which all the nations of Indians were coming home, but, as the messiah looked at the land which was created and reached across the ocean, again disappeared, saying that it was not time for that to take place. The messiah then gave to Good Thunder some paints - Indian paint and a white paint - a green grass [sagebrush twigs?]; and said, 'My grandchildren, when you get home, go to farming and send all your children to school . . . My father commanded me to visit the Indians on a purpose. I have came to the white people first, but they not good. They killed me, and you can see the marks of my wounds on my feet, my hands and my back. My father has given you life - your old life - and you have come to see your friends, but you will not take me home with you at this time. I want you to tell when you get home your people to follow my examples. Any one Indian does not obey me and tries to be on white's side will be covered over by a new land that is to come over this old one. You will, all the people, use the paints and grass I give you. In the spring when the green grass comes, your people who have gone before you will come back and you shall see your friends then, for you have come to my call.'"

"The people from every tipi send for us to visit them. They are people who died many years ago. Chasing Hawk, who died not long ago, was there, and went to his tipi. He was living with his wife, who was killed in war long ago. They live in a buffalo skin tipi - a very large one - and he wanted all his friends to go there to live. A son of Good Thunder who died in war long ago was one who also took us to his tipi so his father saw him . . . "

The Ghost-Dance Religion and Wounded Knee,
Chapter Ten, Appendix, Porcupine's Visit to Wovoka,
By James Mooney, Dover, (Original Publication)
1896, (Tribal: Ghost Dance Religion, Oglala Sioux)

Death According to the Navaho and Pueblo Indians

"At the instant of death the 'soul' escapes the body at the crown of the head, the scalp-lock over the sagittal suture where the two parietal bones articulate."

"But this 'soul' is a dual bi-polar phenomena. Its dark earth-bound principle, the freed anima, hovers around the body for four days. Then it disintegrates and returns to earth - or as the Navajos believe, goes to the symbolic black north. Hence to appease and dismiss it, the various scalp dance ceremonies common to the Pueblos and Navahos. This is the Navaho chindi, the Chinese kuei and the Buddhists' so-called 'astral body,' a nebulous pattern of the whole which is also held to disintegrate after four days."

"Differentiated from this 'ghost' is the enduring life principle, the higher spiritual soul, the bright and active animus. It rises into the air in a superconscious condition and flows back into the reservoir of life. It is this 'spirit' which eventually at the end of the Road of Life will return to 'live in the sun.'"

Hence at Acoma, when a person dies, his hair is parted over the forehead to represent the Milky Way, and the bangs cut with four corners in observance of the ceremonial four day period immediately following death. At the side of the head are placed feathers of the sun hawk and corn husks to show that he has been initiated as a kachina. The body is 'planted' (buried) with the head to the east so he will be reborn. For his spiritual consciousness still has three more worlds or states of existence to pass through. And it is with its experiences that we are now concerned."

"The 'dead' person after he dies, then, undergoes first a four-day period of unconsciousness. It is an embryonic state preceding birth into the after-death world which parallels the embryonic state preceding birth into the human world He then wakes in the Bardo, after-death, dream or subconscious plane to which he has transferred his existence from the mortal, conscious plane. But all his experiences seem as real, as vivid to him as had those in his equally illusory 'living' state."

"They begin at once. According to the Bardo Thodol, he hears a series of four-awe-inspiring' sounds. A sound 'as of a jungle afire'; a sound 'like a thousand thunders reverberating simultaneously'; a sound 'like the breaking of ocean waves'; a sound 'like the crumbling down of a mountain.' It is as if the world is disintegrating around him. His mortal body is. It is beginning to disintegrate and separate into the original elements of the four worlds of which it was composed; fire, air, water, earth . . . "

"But each of these physical elements has its mental and emotional attributes. So now begins a series of psychic experiences. There appear masses of light corresponding to the colors of the four worlds, which blind and dazzle him. Fearful figures which beset him. Wrathful deities which menace him. Peaceful deities which help him. Scenes of violent action which take place before him. These phenomena of course are but psychic reflections of his deeds, thoughts and emotions in previous states. A reading, as it were, of his Book of Memory."

"From some figures and colors he flees; toward some he is inclined . . . He thus follows a colored light path, white, yellow, red, or blue-green, to a corresponding realm or lake. These lakes are synonymous with the Eastern, Southern, Western, or Northern continents, previously described, into which he will be reborn to continue his road. They symbolize the state of development to which he is fitted."

"In these lake realms he leads for a necessary time in his after-death state the life of what we variously term fairies, spirits; the Pueblos as kachinas; the Buddhists as devas. In the fourth dimensional existence all these beings of like inclination, development, and destination live consciously together, see each other with deva vision, just as they did in their incarnate world existence. But they cannot be seen by those of dissimilar orders, nor by man. They may pay visits to help mankind, but they are not gods . . . "

"So it is from here that the kachinas come - these 'many ladies and gentlemen, pleasant, courteous, and respectful' . . . They are the spirits of the dead . . . "

"And why have they come? Why simply to recount their story to fellow travelers whom they have 'passed on their roads,' and to assure them of an equally pleasant journey . . . Above all, to reassure their people of the naturalness of the death process and death state as paralleling their existence on earth . . . it reaffirms a belief in the ultimate evolution of

every living thing . . ."
Masked Gods, Chapter 7, Page 300-302, By Frank Waters, Ballantine, 1950, (Native American: Navajo/Pueblo)

Auspicious Experience of the Cheyenne/Arapahoe Visionquest

"You feel a chill. You open your eyes and see the sun going down. You most to the western point of your circle and offer your pipe and sacred smoke to the setting sun. Then you move back to the center of your circle, lie down and wrap yourself in your blanket. You place your pipe on the ground, at arm's length, with its stem pointing East, ready to greet the rising sun of the forthcoming day. Flocks of blue jays hustle to a grove of cedars to bed down for the night. Nighthawks begin to nosedive and soar in all directions. You behold. You are attentive."

After awhile you feel like there is sawdust in your eyes and you decide to sleep. It has been a full day. You have fasted and sweat, both in prayer and in ceremony, both in celebration and preparation. Tomorrow you will greet the rising sun and the morning star. Tomorrow you will be out, all day, alone, yet not alone, from sunrise till sunset. You will stay in your circle out on this hill in this hidden valley."

"You pray for guidance to come in your dreams . . . As you close your eyes ready to sleep, the nighthawks dive down closer to you. You call out, 'Aho brothers.' Tonight is a good night to sleep and to dream."

Breath of the Invisible, Chapter Six, The Vision Quest, Page 44, By John Redtail Freesoul, Quest Books, 1986, (Native American: Cheyenne/Arapahoe)

Auspicious Medicine of the Wahpeton Dakota

"According to the Wahpeton Dakota, their medicine men lived a prenatal existence among the Thunders and enjoyed a knowledge, prior to birth, of all that would happen to them as mortals. Their social role began with maturity, when they received a sign from the Thunders to start performing shamanistic duties; any shaman disobeying the divine orders would suffer punishment or even be killed by the Thunders."

Indians of the Plains, Chapter 6, Page 176, By Robert Lowie, American Museum Science Books, 1954, (Native American: Wahpeton Dakota)

Auspicious Experience of Black Elk

Black Elk
*("The Sacred Pipe," Recorded by Joseph Epes Brown, Photograph by
J.E. Brown, University of Oklahoma Press, 1953)*

"While I was eating, a voice came and said: 'It is time; now they are calling you.' The voice was so loud and clear that I believed it, and I thought I would just go where it wanted me to go. So I got right up and started. As I came out of the teepee, both my thighs began to hurt me, and suddenly it was like waking from a dream, and there wasn't any voice. So I went back into the tepee . . . I could see out through the opening, and there two men were coming from the clouds, head-first like arrows slanting down, and I knew they were the same that I had seen before. Each now carried a long spear, and from the points of these a jagged lightning flashed. They came clear down to the ground this time and stood a little way off and looked at me and said: 'Hurry! Come! Your Grandfathers are calling you!'"

*Black Elk Speaks, Chapter III, The Great Vision, By
John G. Neihardt, (Native American: Oglala Sioux)*

Auspicious Words of Chief Joseph

Chief Joseph
("I Will Fight no More Forever," By Merrill D. Beal, Photograph by
Historical Society of Montana,
Ballantine Walden, 1963)

"I am tired of fighting. Our chiefs are killed. Looking Glass is dead. Toohulhulsote is dead. The old men are all dead. It is the young men who say yes or no. He who led the young men is dead. It is cold and we have no blankets. The little children are freezing to death. My people, some of them, have run away to the hills and have no blankets, no food. No one knows where they are - perhaps freezing to death. I want to have time to look for my children and see how many of them I can find. Maybe I shall find them among the dead. Hear me, my chiefs. I am tired. My heart is sick and sad. From where the sun now stands

I will fight no more forever."
*The Ghost-Dance Religion and Wounded Knee,
Chapter Six, Character of the Nez Perces, By James
Mooney, Dover, (Original Publication) 1896, (Tribal:
Ghost Dance Religion, Oglala Sioux)*

CHAPTER EIGHT
ISLAM

Mohammed   **Mohammed with the Angel**
(*" Religions of the World,"* Page 431, The Granger Collection, By St.
Martin's Press, 1993) AND (*"Great Religions of the World,"* By the
National Geographic Society, 1971)

Auspicious Birth of Muhammed the Prophet

The Prophet Muhammed is said to have been
born around 570 A.D. in Quraysh, Mecca to a poor
family. His father had died before he was born and
his mother in his early childhood. Raised by an Uncle,
Abu Talib, Muhammed was not to receive his call
until he was 40 years of age.

"Rabia b. Nasr, king of the Yaman . . . had a
vision which terrified him and continued to cause
him much anxiety. So he summoned every

soothsayer, sorcerer, omenmonger and astrologer in his kingdom and said: 'I have had a vision which terrifies me and is a source of anxiety. Tell me what it was and what it means.' They replied: 'Tell us the vision and we will tell you its meaning.' 'If I tell you it,' said he, 'I can have no confidence in your interpretation; for the only man who knows its meaning is he who knows about the vision without my telling him.' Thereupon one of them recommended him to send for Shiqq and Satih, for they knew more than others and would be able to answer his questions . . . So he sent for them and Satih arrived first."

After accurately retelling and interpreting the terrifying dream which foresaw much bloodshed, war and the conquering of the king's land by another army, he went on to say these words:

"His kingdom shall be ended by an apostle who will bring truth and justice among men of religion and virtue. Dominion will rest among his people until the Day of Separation, the day on which those near God will be rewarded, on which demands from heaven will be made which the quick and the dead will hear, men will be gathered at the appointed place, the God-fearing to receive salvation and blessing. By the Lord of heaven and earth, and what lies between them high or low I have told you but the truth in which no doubt lies."

The Life of Muhammad, Translation of Ishaq's Sirat Rasul Allah, Part I, The Genealogy of Muhammad, Of Rabi'a B. Nasr King of the Yaman and the Story of Shiqq and Satih the Two Soothsayers, 9-12, Oxford University Press, Introduction and Notes by A.

Guillaume (Islam)

"It is alleged in popular stories (and only God knows the truth) that Amina D. Wahb, the mother of God's apostle, used to say when she was pregnant with God's apostle that a voice said to her, 'You are pregnant with the Lord of this people and when he is born say, 'I put him in the care of the One from the evil of every envier; then call him Muhammad." As she was pregnant with him she saw a light come forth from her by which she could see the castles of Busra in Syria. Shortly afterwards, Abdullah the apostle's father died while his mother was still pregnant."

The Life of Muhammad, Translation of Ishaq's Sirat Rasul Allah, Part I, The Genealogy of Muhammad, What Was Said to Amina When She Had Conceived the Apostle, 102, Oxford University Press, Introduction and Notes by A. Guillaume, (Islam)

"Halima the apostle's foster-mother used to say that she went forth from her country with her husband and little son whom she was nursing, among the women of her tribe, in search of other babies to nurse. This was a year of famine when they were destitute. She was riding a dusky she-donkey of hers with an old she-camel which did not yield a drop of milk. They could not sleep the whole night because of the weeping of her hungry child. She had no milk to give him, nor could their she-camel provide a morning draught, but were hoping for rain and relief. 'I rode upon my donkey which had kept back the other riders through its weakness and emaciation so that it was a nuisance to them. When we reached

Mecca, we looked out for foster children, and the apostle of God was offered to everyone of us, and each woman refused him when she was told he was an orphan, because we hoped to get payment from the child's father. We said, 'An orphan! And what will his mother and grandmother do?', and so we spurned him because of that. Every woman who came with me got a suckling except me, and when we decided to depart I said to my husband: 'By God, I do not like the idea of returning with my friends without a suckling; I will go and take that orphan.' He replied, 'Do as you please, perhaps God will bless us on this account. So I went and took him for the sole reason that I could not find anyone else. I took him back to my baggage, and as soon as I put him in my bosom, my breasts overflowed with milk which he drank until he was satisfied, as also did his foster-brother. Then both of them slept, whereas before this we could not sleep with him. My husband got up and went to the old she-camel and lo, her udders were full; he milked it and he and I drank of her milk until we were completely satisfied, and we passed a happy night. In the morning my husband said: 'Do you know, Halima, you have taken a blessed creature?' I said, 'By God, I hope so.' Then we set out and I was riding my she-ass and carrying him with me, and she went at such a pace that the other donkeys could not keep up so that my companions said to me, 'Confound you! Stop and wait for us. Isn't this the donkey on which you started?' 'Certainly, it is,' I said. They replied, 'By God, something extraordinary has happened.' Then we came to our dwellings in the Banu Sa'd country and I do not know a country more barren than that."

"When we had him with us my flock used to yield milk in abundance. We milked them and drank while other people had not a drop, nor could they find anything in their animals' udders, so that our people were saying to their shepherds, 'Woe to you! Send your flock to graze where the daughter of Abu Dhuayb's shepherd goes.' Even so, their flocks came back hungry not yielding a drop of milk, while mine had milk in abundance. We ceased not to recognize this bounty as coming from God for a period of two years, when I weaned him. He was growing up as none of the other children grew and by the time he was two he was a well-made child. We brought him to his mother, though we were most anxious to keep him with us because of the blessing which he brought us. I said to her: I should like you to leave my little boy with me until he becomes a big boy, for I am afraid on his account of the pest in Mecca.' We persisted until she sent him back with us.'"

"Some months after our return he and his brother were with our lambs behind the tents when his brother came running and said to us, 'Two men clothed in white have seized that Qurayshi brother of mine and thrown him down and opened up his belly, and are stirring it up.' We ran towards him and found him standing up with a livid face. We took hold of him and asked him what was the matter. He said, 'Two men in white raiment came and threw me down and opened up my belly and searched therein for I know not what.' So we took him back to our tent."

"His father said to me, 'I am afraid that this

child has had a stroke, so take him back to his family before the result appears.' So we picked him up and took him to his mother who asked why we had brought him when I had been anxious for his welfare and desirous of keeping him with me. I said to her, 'God has let my son live so far and I have done my duty. I am afraid that ill will befall him, so I have brought him back to you as you wished.' She asked me what happened and gave me no peace until I told her. When she asked if I feared a demon possessed him, I replied that I did. She answered that no demon had any power over her son who had a great future before him, and then she told how when she was pregnant with him a light went out from her which illumined the castles of Busra in Syria, and that she had borne him with the least difficulty imaginable. When she bore him he put his hands on the ground lifting his head towards the heavens. 'Leave him then and go in peace,' she said."

Mohammed later told his companions this:

"When my mother was carrying me she saw a light proceeding from her which showed her the castles of Syria. I was suckled among the B. Sa'd b. Bakr, and while I was with a brother of mine behind our tents shepherding the lambs, two men in white raiment came to me with a gold basin full of snow. Then they seized me and opened up my belly, extracted my heart and split it; then they extracted a black drop from it and threw it away; then they washed my heart and my belly with that snow until they had thoroughly cleaned them. Then one said to the other, weigh him against ten of his people; they did so and I outweighed them. Then they weighed me against a hundred and then a thousand, and I outweighed them. He said, 'Leave him alone, for by God, if you weighed him against all his people he would outweigh them.'"

The Life of Muhammad, Translation of Ishaq's Sirat Rasul Allah, Part I, The Genealogy of Muhammad, The Birth of the Apostle and His Suckling, 104-106, Oxford University Press, Introduction and Notes by A. Guillaume, (Islam)

"A learned person told me that what urged his foster-mother to return him to his mother, apart from what she told his mother, was that a number of Abyssinian Christians saw him with her when she brought him back after he had been weaned. They looked at him, asked questions about him, and studied him carefully, then they said to her, 'Let us take this boy, and bring him to our king and our country; for he will have a great future. We know all about him.' The person who told me this alleged that she could hardly get him away from them."

The Life of Muhammad, Translation of Ishaq's Sirat Rasul Allah, Part I, The Genealogy of Muhammad, The Birth of the Apostle and His Suckling, 107, Oxford University Press, Introduction and Notes by A. Guillaume, (Islam)

"When the caravan reached Busra in Syria, there was a monk there in his cell by the name of Bahira, who was well versed in the knowledge of Christians. A monk had always occupied that cell. There he gained his knowledge from a book that was in the cell, so they allege, handed on from generation to generation. They had often passed by him in the past and he never spoke to them or took any notice of them until this year, and when they stopped near his cell he made a great feast for them. It is alleged that that was because of something he saw while in his cell. They allege that while he was in his cell he saw the apostle of God in the caravan when they approached, with a cloud over-shadowing him among the people. Then they came and stopped in the shadow of a tree near the monk. He looked at the cloud when it overshadowed the tree, and its branches were bending and drooping over the apostle of God until he was in the shadow beneath it. When Bahira saw that, he came out of his cell and sent word to them. 'I have prepared food for you, O men of Quraysh, and I should like you all to come both great and small, bond and free.' One of them said to him, 'By God Bahira! Something extraordinary has happened today, you used not to treat us so, and we have often passed by you. What has befallen you today? He answered 'You are right in what you say, but you are guests and I wish to honour you and give you food so that you may eat.' So they gathered together with him, leaving the Apostle of God behind with the baggage under the tree, on account of his extreme youth. When Bahira looked at the people he did not see the mark which he knew and found in his books, so he said, 'Do not let one of you remain behind and not come to my feast,' . . . Thereupon he told them to invite him to come to the meal with them . . . Then he got up and embraced him and made him sit with the people. When Bahira saw him he stared at him closely, looking at his body and finding traces of his description (in the Christian books). When the people had finished eating and gone away, Bahira got up and said to him, 'Boy, I ask you by al-Lat and al-Uzza to answer my question.' Now Bahira said this only because he had heard his people swearing by these gods. They allege that the apostle of God said to him, 'Do not ask me by al-Lat and al-Uzza, for by Allah nothing is more hateful to me than these two.' Bahira answered, 'Then by Allah, tell me what I ask'; he replied, 'Ask me what you like; so he began to ask him about what happened in his (T. waking and in his) sleep, and his habits, and his affairs generally, and what the apostle of God told him coincided with what Bahira knew of his description. Then he looked at his back and saw the seal of prophethood between his shoulders in the very place described in his book (123). When he had finished he went to his uncle Abu Talib and asked him what relation this boy was to him, and when he told him he was his son, he said that he was not, for it could not be that the father of this boy was alive. 'He is my nephew,' he said, and when he asked what had become of his father he told him that he had died before the child was born. 'You have told the truth,' said Bahira, 'Take your nephew back to his country and guard him carefully against the Jews, for by Allah! If they see him and know about him what I know, they will do him evil; a great future lies before this nephew of yours, so take him home quickly.'"

The Life of Muhammad, Translation of Ishaq's Sirat

Rasul Allah, Part I, The Genealogy of Muhammad,
The Story of Bahira, 115-117, Oxford University
Press, Introduction and Notes by A. Guillaume,
(Islam)

"The apostle stopped in the shade of a tree near a monk's cell, when the monk came up to Maysara and asked who the man was who was resting beneath the tree. He told him that he was of Quraysh, the people who held the sanctuary; and the monk exclaimed: 'None but a prophet ever sat beneath this tree.'"

" . . . The story goes that at the height of noon when the heat was intense as he rode his beast Maysara saw two angels shading the apostle from the suns's rays."

The Life of Muhammad, Translation of Ishaq's Sirat
Rasul Allah, Part I, The Genealogy of Muhammad,
The Apostle of God Marries Khadija (126), 119-120,
Oxford University Press, Introduction and Notes by
A. Guillaume, (Islam)

Auspicious Experiences of the Prophet Muhammed

"He then completed the prayer as it was required to complete and the sun brightened and he said: O people! verily the sun and the moon are among the signs of Allah and they do not eclipse at the death of anyone among people (Abu Bakr said: On the death of any human being). So when you see anything like it (of the nature of the eclipse), pray till it is bright. There is nothing which you have been promised (in the next world) but I have seen it in this prayer of mine. Hell was brought to me as you saw me moving back on account of fear lest its heat might affect me . . . Paradise was brought to me, and it was on that occasion that you saw me moving forward till I stood at my place (of worship). I stretched my hand as I wanted to catch hold of its fruits so that you may see them. Then I thought of not doing it. Nothing which you have been promised was there that I did not see in this prayer of mine."

" . . . There was no such thing as I did not see earlier, but I saw it at this very place of mine. I ever saw Paradise and Hell. It was also revealed to me that you would be tried in the graves . . . "

Sahih Muslim, Volume II, Kitab-Al Salat, Chapter CCCXXII, (No. 1976-1977), Translated by Abdul Hamid Siddiqi, Kitab Bhavan, New Delhi-110002, (Islam)

"He then observed prostration, and then he finished, and the sun had cleared (by that time) . . . They (his Companions) said: Messenger of Allah, we saw you reach out to something, while you were standing here; then we saw you restrain yourself. He said: I saw Paradise and reached out to a bunch of its grapes; and had I taken it you would have eaten of it as long as the world endured. I saw Hell also. No such (abominable) sight have I ever seen as that which I saw today; and I observed that most of its inhabitants were women. They said: Messenger of Allah, on what account is it so? He said: For their ingratitude or disbelief (bi-kufraihinna). It was said:

Do they disbelieve in Allah? He said: (Not for their disbelief in God) but for their ingratitude to their husbands and ingratitude to kindness. If you were to treat one of them kindly for ever, but if she later saw anything (displeasing) in you, she would say: I have never seen any good in you."

Sahih Muslim, Volume II, Kitab-Al Salat, Chapter CCCXXII, (No. 1982), Translated by Abdul Hamid Siddiqi, Kitab Bhavan, New Delhi-110002, (Islam)

Auspicious Death of the Prophet Muhammed

"In the middle of the night the apostle sent for me and told me that he was ordered to pray for the dead in this cemetery and that I was to go with him. I went; and when he stood among them he said, 'Peace upon you, O people of the graves! Happy are you that you are so much better off than men here. Dissensions have come like waves of darkness one after the other, the last being worse than the first.' Then he turned to me and said, 'I have been given the choice between the keys of the treasuries of this world and long life here followed by Paradise, and meeting my Lord and Paradise (at once).' I urged him to choose the former, but he said that he had chosen the latter. Then he prayed for the dead there and went away. Then it was that the illness through which God took him began. "

The Life of Muhammad, Translation of Ishaq's Sirat Rasul Allah, Part III, The Beginning of the Apostle's Illness, 1000, Oxford University Press, Introduction and Notes by A. Guillaume, (Islam)

"Ibn Shihab al-Zuhri told me from 'Ubayd b. 'Abdullah b. 'Utba from A'isha that she used to hear the apostle say, 'God never takes a prophet to Himself without giving him the choice.' When he was at the point of death the last word I heard the apostle saying was, 'Nay, rather the Exalted Companion of paradise.' I said (to myself), 'Then by God he is not choosing us!' And I knew that that was what he used to tell us, namely that a prophet does not die without being given the choice."

The Life of Muhammad, Translation of Ishaq's Sirat Rasul Allah, Part III, The Apostle's Illness in the House of A'isha, 1008, Oxford University Press, Introduction and Notes by A. Guillaume, (Islam)

"I found him heavy in my bosom and as I looked into his face, lo his eyes were fixed and he was saying, 'Nay, the most Exalted Companion is of paradise.' I said, 'You were given the choice and you have chosen, by Him Who sent you with the truth!'" And so the apostle was taken . . . He (Abu Bakr) went and uncovered his face and kissed him, saying, 'You are dearer than my father and mother. You have tasted the death which God had decreed: a second death will never overtake you.' Then he replaced the mantle on the apostle's face and went out. Umar was still speaking and he said, 'Gently, 'Umar, be quiet.' But 'Umar refused and went on talking, and when Abu Bakr saw that he would not be silent he went forward to the people who, when they heard his words, came to him and left 'Umar. Giving thanks and praise to God he said: 'O men, if anyone worships

Muhammad, Muhammad is dead: if anyone worships God, God is alive, immortal.' Then he recited this verse: 'Muhammad is nothing but an apostle. Apostles have passed away before him. Can it be that if he were to die or be killed you would turn back on your heels?'"

The Life of Muhammad, Translation of Ishaq's Sirat Rasul Allah, Part III, The Apostle's Illness in the House of A'isha, 1012, Oxford University Press, Introduction and Notes by A. Guillaume, (Islam)

Death According to the Prophet Muhammed

"I asked: 'O Apostle of Allah, what will our Lord do with us when we meet Him?'"

"He replied: 'You will be exposed to Him and all your sides will be manifest to Him. Nothing of you will remain concealed from Him. Then your Lord, (the Mighty and the Exalted), will take up a handful of water and sprinkle it on you. By the name of your Lord, no face of yours will miss a drop of it.'"

"'As a result, it will leave the face of the Muslim like a white sheet; but as regards the infidel it will burn him thoroughly like black charcoals.'"

"'Behold, then your Prophet will depart and the good ones will follow him. Then they will come across a bridge of fire; every one of you stepping on the charcoal and saying 'Oh!' Your Lord, (the Mighty and Great), will say: 'Yes' (now is the proper time).'"

"'Lo, then you will come on the 'Haud' (pool of water) of your Prophet with an extreme thirst for a draught of water which, by Allah, I have never seen.'"

"'By the name of Allah, none of you will stretch out his hand but a cup of water will come down to him which will purify him from ordure, urine, and other unclean things.'"

"'And the sun and the moon will be concealed such as you will not see either of the two.'"

"I said: 'O Apostle of Allah, then how shall we see?' He replied: (You will see) as you see just now. It is as you do with the sunrise on a particular day when the earth is shining and the hills have come inbetween.' I enquired: 'O Apostle of Allah, how will our evil and good deeds be requited?' He replied: 'The good deeds (will be requited) ten times and the bad deeds one time, save He forgives.' I inquired: 'O Apostle of Allah, what are the Heaven and the Hell?' He answered: 'By the name of your Allah, verily the Hell has got seven gates; there are no two gates but a horseman can travel between them for seventy years. And the Heaven has got eight gates; between any two gates the horseman can travel for seventy years.' I asked: 'O Apostle of Allah, upon which part of the Heaven shall we appear?' He replied: 'Upon rivers of pure honey, streams of wine having in it no headache and regret; streams of milk, the taste of which will not be altered; of water which is not stagnant; and upon fruits; and by the name of your Lord, upon something better than this which you do now know.'"

The Orations of Muhammad, Translated by Muhammad Abaidul Akbar, Page 65-68, Sh. Muhammad Ashraf Publishers, 1954, (Islam, Words of Muhammed)

Sufi Crossing the Water on a Prayer Mat (Rumi)
(*"Religions of the World,"* Page 476, *The Granger Collection, From a Moghul book of 1629, St. Martin's Press, 1993*)

"The son of Mary, Jesus, hurries up a slope as though a wild animal were chasing him. Someone following him asks, 'Where are you going? No one is after you.' Jesus keeps on, saying nothing, across two more fields. 'Are you the one who says words over a dead person, so that he wakes up?' I am. 'Did you not make the clay birds fly?' Yes. 'Who then could possibly cause you to run like this?' Jesus slows his pace. 'I say the Great Name over the deaf and the blind, they are healed. Over a stony mountainside, and it tears its mantle down to the navel. Over non-existence, it comes into existence. But when I speak lovingly for hours, for days, with those who take human warmth and mock it, when I say the Name to them, nothing happens. They remain rock, or turn to sand, where no plants can grow. Other diseases are ways for mercy to enter, but this non-responding breeds violence and coldness towards God. I am fleeing from that. As little by little air steals water, so praise dries up and evaporates with foolish people who refuse to change. Like cold stone you sit on a cynic steals body heat. He doesn't feel the sun.' Jesus wasn't running away from actual people. He was teaching in a new way."

The Essential Rumi, Chapter 19, What Jesus Runs Away From, Translated by Coleman Barks, Harper SanFrancisco 1995, (Islam: Sufi, Words of Rumi)

Death According to the Sufi Prophet Rumi

"A lover was telling his beloved how much he loved her, how faithful he had been, how self-sacrificing, getting up at dawn every morning, fasting, giving up wealth and strength and fame, all for her."

"There was a fire in him. He didn't know where it came from, but it made him weep and melt like a candle. 'You've done well,' she said, 'but listen to me. All this is the decor of love, the branches and leaves and blossoms. You must live at the root to be a true lover.' 'Where is that! Tell me!' 'You've done the outward acts, but you haven't died. You must die.'"

"When he heard that, he lay back on the ground laughing, and died. He opened like a rose that drops to the ground and died laughing. That laughter was his freedom, and his gift to the eternal. As moonlight shines back at the sun, he heard the call to come home, and went. When light returns to its source, it takes nothing of what it has illuminated. It may have shone on a garbage dump, or a garden, or in the center of a human eye. No matter. It goes, and when it does, the open plain becomes passionately desolate, wanting it back."

The Essential Rumi, Chapter 20, Dying, Laughing, Translated by Coleman Barks, Harper SanFrancisco 1995, (Islam: Sufi, Words of Rumi)

"This moment this love comes to rest in me, many beings in one being. In one wheat grain a thousand sheaf stacks. Inside the needle's eye a turning night of stars. Keep walking, though there's no place to get to. Don't try to see through the distances. That's not for human beings. Move within, but don't move the way fear makes you move . . . I am so small I can barely be seen. How can this great love be inside me? Look at your eyes. They are small, but they see enormous things . . . Whoever finds love beneath hurt and grief disappears into emptiness with a thousand new disguises. Dance, when you're broken open. Dance, if you've torn the bandage off. Dance in the middle of fighting. Dance in your blood. Dance, when you're perfectly free."

The Essential Rumi, Chapter 27, Various Stanzas, Translated by Coleman Barks, Harper SanFrancisco 1995, (Islam: Sufi, Words of Rumi)

183

CHAPTER NINE
BAHA'I

Auspicious Birth of the Bab', Forerunner of Baha'u'llah the Prophet

The Forerunner of the Prophet Baha'u'llah, the Bab', is said to have been born on the 20th of October, 1819 - named Mirza Ali Muhammad - in Shiraz, the South of Persia to a fairly well-to-do family. A Siyyid (Descendant of the Prophet Muhammed), his father died shortly after his birth. He received his call when he was 25 years of age.

"What he intended by the term Bab was this, that he was a channel of grace from some great Person still behind the veil of glory, who was the possessor of countless and boundless perfections, by whose will he moved, and to the bond of whose love he clung."
A Traveler's Narrative, Page 3, Baha'i Publishing Trust, 1980, Abdu'l-Baha (Baha'i, Words of Baha'u'llah)

Auspicious Birth of Baha'u'llah the Prophet

The Prophet Baha'u'llah is said to have been born on the 12th of November, 1817 - named Mirza Husayn-'Ali - in the village of Takur in the district of Nur (Light) in the northern province of Mazindran to a fairly well-to-do family. Baha'u'llah received his call when he was 27 years of age.

"At the age of five or six Husayn-Ali had dreams which he related to his father, describing a desert garden in which huge birds were attacking him from every side but without harming him; and he told also of swimming in waters where birds of the air and fishes of the sea were attacking him while he remained unscathed. The Vazir called upon a famous seer who explained the visions as indicating that the child would become the founder of a great cause and that, despite the attacks of the leaders and the learned of the world, the birds and the fishes of the dream, no harm would come to him but rather that he would be victorious over all."

Robe of Light, The Celestial Tree Grows, Page 26,
David S. Ruhe, George Ronald Publishers, 1994,
(Baha'i)

"When Baha'u'llah was still a child, the Vazir, His father, dreamed a dream. Baha'u'llah appeared to him swimming in a vast, limitless ocean. His body shone upon the waters with a radiance that illumined the sea. Around his head, which could distinctly be seen above the waters, there radiated, in all directions, His long, jet-black locks, floating in great profusion above the waves. As he dreamed, a multitude of fishes gathered round Him, each holding fast to the extremity of one hair. Fascinated by the effulgence of His face, they followed Him in whatever direction He swam. Great as was their number, and however firmly they clung to His locks, not one single hair seemed to have been detached from His head, nor did the least injury affect His person. Free and unrestrained, He moved above the waters and they all followed Him."

"The Vazir, greatly impressed by this dream, summoned a soothsayer, who had achieved fame in that region, and asked him to interpret it for him. This man, as if inspired by a premonition of the future glory of Baha'u'llah, declared: 'The limitless ocean that you have seen in your dream, O Vazir, is none other than the world of being. Single-handed and alone, your son will achieve supreme ascendancy over it. Wherever He may please, He will proceed unhindered. No one will resist His march, no one will hinder his progress. The Multitude of fishes signifies the turmoil which He will arouse amidst the peoples and kindreds of the earth. Around Him will they gather, and to Him will they cling. Assured of the unfailing protection of the Almighty, this tumult will never harm His person, nor will His loneliness upon the sea of life endanger His safety.'"

"That soothsayer was subsequently taken to see Baha'u'llah. He looked intently upon His face, and examined carefully His features. He was charmed by His appearance, and extolled every trait of His countenance. Every expression in that face revealed to his eyes a sign of His concealed glory. So great was his admiration, and so profuse his praise of Baha'u'llah, that the Vazir, from that day, became even more passionately devoted to his son. The words spoken by that soothsayer served to fortify his hopes

and confidence in Him. Like Jacob, he desired only to ensure the welfare of his beloved Joseph, and to surround Him with his loving protection."
Nabil 3, The Call to Remembrance, Childhood, Baha'i Publishing Trust, 1992, Compiled by Geoffry W. Marks (Baha'i)

"When He was only thirteen or fourteen years old He became renowned for His learning. He would converse on any subject and solve any problem presented to Him. In large gatherings He would discuss matters with the Ulama (leading mulla's) and would explain intricate religious questions. All of them used to listen to Him with the greatest interest.
Abdu'l-Baha 4, The Call to Remembrance, Childhood, Baha'i Publishing Trust, 1992, Compiled by Geoffry W. Marks (Baha'i)

"Shaykh Muhammad-Taqi related to his disciples two of his recent dreams, the details of which he believed were of utmost significance."
"'In my first dream,' he began, 'I was standing in the midst of a vast concourse of people, all of whom seemed to be pointing to a certain house in which they said the (Lord of the Age) dwelt. Frantic with joy, I hastened in my dream to attain His presence. When I reached the house, I was, to my great surprise, refused admittance. 'The promised qa'im', I was informed, 'is engaged in private conversation with another person. Access to them is strictly forbidden.' From the guards who were standing beside the door, I gathered that that person was none other than Husayn-Ali.'"

"Of the second dream, the Shaykh recounted that he came upon a room filled with chests which, he was told, belonged to Mirza Husayn-Ali. On opening one, he found it packed with books, all of whose lines were studded with gems, their brilliance awakening him."
Robe of Light, The Celestial Tree Grows, Page 34, David S. Ruhe, George Ronald Publishers, 1994, (Baha'i)

Auspicious Experience of the Bab', Forerunner of the Prophet Baha'u'llah

" . . . my conductor paused for a moment while I removed my shoes. Then, with a quick movement of the hand, he withdrew, and, as I passed, replaced the curtain; and I found myself in a large apartment, along the upper end of which ran a low divan, while on the side opposite to the door were placed two or three chairs. Though I dimly suspected whither I was going and whom I was to behold (for no distinct intimation had been given to me), a second or two elapsed ere, with a throb of wonder and awe, I became definitely conscious that the room was not untenanted. In the corner where the divan met the wall sat a wondrous and venerable figure, crowned with a felt head-dress of the kind called taj by dervishes (but of unusual height and make), round the base of which was wound a small white turban. The face of him on whom I gazed I can never forget, though I cannot describe it. Those piercing eyes seemed to read one's very soul' power and authority sat on that ample brow; while the deep lines on the forehead and face implied an age which the jet-black hair and beard flowing down in indistinguishable luxuriance almost to the waist seemed to belie. No need to ask in whose presence I stood, as I bowed myself before one who is the object of a devotion and love which kings might envy and emperors sigh for in vain!"

"A mild dignified voice bade me be seated, and then continued: - 'Praise be to God that thou hast attained! . . . Thou has come to see a prisoner and an exile . . . We desire but the good of the world and happiness of the nations; yet they deem us a stirrer up of strife and sedition worthy of bondage and banishment . . . That all nations should become one in faith and all men as brothers; that the bonds of affection and unity between the sons of men should be strengthened; that diversity of religion should cease, and differences of race be annulled - - what harm is there in this? . . . Yet so it shall be; these fruitless strifes, these ruinous wars shall pass away, and the 'Most Great Peace' shall come . . . Do not you in Europe need this also? Is not this that which Christ foretold? . . . Yet do we see your kings and rulers lavishing their treasures more freely on means for the destruction of the human race than on that which would conduce to the happiness of mankind . . . These strifes and this bloodshed and discord must cease, and all men be as one kindred and one family . . . Let not a man glory in this, that he loves his country; let him rather glory in this, that he loves his kind . . . '"

"Such, so far as I can recall them, were the words which, besides many other, I heard from Beha. Let those who read them consider well with themselves whether such doctrines merit death and bonds, and whether the world is more likely to gain or lose by their diffusion. "

A Traveler's Narrative, Introduction, Baha'i Publishing Trust, 1980, Abdu'l-Baha (Baha'i, Words of Baha'u'llah)

Auspicious Experiences of the Prophet Baha'u'llah

"I was asleep on My couch: the breaths of My Lord the Merciful passed over Me and awakened Me from sleep: to this bear witness the denizens (of the realms) of His Power and His Kingdom, and the dwellers in the cities of His Glory, and Himself, the True. I am not impatient of calamities in His way, nor of afflictions for His love and at His good pleasure. God hath made affliction as a morning shower to this green pasture, and as a match for His lamp whereby earth and heaven are illumined."

A Traveler's Narrative, Page 77, Baha'i Publishing Trust, 1980, Abdu'l-Baha (Baha'i, Words of Baha'u'llah)

"One night, in a dream, these exalted words were heard on every side. 'Verily, We shall render Thee victorious by Thyself or by Thy Pen. Grieve Thou not for that which hath befallen Thee, neither be

Thou afraid, for Thou art in safety. Erelong will God raise up the treasures of the earth-men who will aid Thee through Thyself and through Thy Name, wherewith God hath revived the hearts of such as have recognized Him."

Epistle to the Son of the Wolf, Page 20-21, Baha'i Publishing Trust, 1941, Baha'u'llah, (Baha'i, Words of Baha'ullah)

Auspicious Death of the Bab, Forerunner of Baha'u'llah the Prophet

"On the 9th of July, 1850, the Bab Himself, Who was then in His thirty-first year, fell a victim to the fanatical fury of His persecutors. With a devoted young follower named Aqa Muhammad Ali, who had passionately begged to be allowed to share His martyrdom, He was led to the scaffold in the old barrack square of Tabriz. About two hours before noon the two were suspended by ropes under their armpits in such a way that the head of Muhammad Ali rested against the breast of his beloved Master. A regiment of Armenian soldiers was drawn up and received the order to fire. Promptly the volleys rang out, but when the smoke cleared, it was found that the Bab and His companion were still alive. The bullets had but severed the ropes by which they were suspended, so that they dropped to the ground unhurt. The Bab proceeded to a room nearby where he was found talking to one of his friends. About noon they were again suspended. The Armenians,

who considered the result of their volleys a miracle, were unwilling to fire again, so another regiment of soldiers had been brought on the scene, who fired when ordered. This time the volleys took effect."
Baha'u'llah and the New Era, The Bab: The Forerunner, Page 17-18, Baha'i Publishing Trust, 1950, (Baha'i)

Auspicious Death of the Prophet Baha'u'llah

"Already nine months before His ascension Baha'u'llah, as attested to Abdu'l-Baha, had voiced His desire to depart from this world. From that time onward it became increasingly evident, from the tone of His remarks to those who attained His presence, that the close of His earthly life was approaching, though He refrained from mentioning it openly to anyone. On the night preceding the eleventh of Shavva'l 1309 A.H. (May 8, 1892) He contracted a slight fever which, though it mounted the following day, soon after subsided. He continued to grant interviews to certain of the friends and pilgrims, but it soon became evident that He was not well. His fever returned in a more acute form than before, His general condition grew steadily worse, complications ensued which at last culminated in His ascension, at the hour of dawn, on the 2nd of Dhi'l-Qa'dih 1309 A.H. (May 29, 1892), eight hours after sunset, in the 75th year of his age. His spirit, at long last released from the toils of a life crowded with tribulations, had winged its flight to His "other dominions,' dominions "whereon the eyes of the people of names have never fallen," and to which the "Luminous maid," "clad in white," had bidden Him hasten, as described by Himself in the Lawh-i-Ru'ya' (Tablet of the Vision), revealed nineteen years previously, on the anniversary of the birth of His Forerunner. "

" . . . The inconsolable Nabil, who had had the privilege of a private audience with Baha'u'llah during the days of His illness; whom Abdu'l-Baha had chosen to select those passages which constitute the text of the Tablet of Visitation now recited in the Most Holy Tomb; and who, in his uncontrollable grief, drowned himself in the sea shortly after the passing of his Beloved, thus describes the agony of those days: 'Methinks, the spiritual commotion set up in the world of dust had caused all the worlds of God to tremble . . . My inner and outer tongue are powerless to portray the condition we were in . . . In the midst of the prevailing confusion a multitude of the inhabitants of Akka and of the neighboring villages, that had thronged the fields surrounding the Mansion, could be seen weeping, beating upon their heads, and crying aloud their grief.'"

*God Passes By, Ascension of Baha'u'llah, Baha'i
Publishing Trust, 1944, Shoghi Effendi (Baha'i)*

Death According to the Prophet Baha'u'llah

"And now concerning thy question regarding the soul of man and its survival after death. Know thou of a truth that the soul, after its separation from the body, will continue to progress until it attaineth the presence of God, in a state and condition which neither the revolution of ages and centuries, nor the changes and chances of this world, can alter. It will endure as long as the Kingdom of God, His sovereignty, His dominion and power will endure. It will manifest the signs of God and His attributes, and will reveal His loving-kindness and bounty. The movement of My Pen is stilled when it attempteth to befittingly describe the loftiness and glory of so exalted a station. The honor with which the Hand of Mercy will invest the soul is such as no tongue can adequately reveal, nor any other earthly agency describe. Blessed is the soul which, at the hour of its separation from the body, is sanctified from the vain imaginings of the peoples of the world. Such a soul liveth and moveth in accordance with the Will of its Creator, and entereth the all-highest Paradise. The Maids of Heaven, inmates of the loftiest mansions, will circle around it, and the Prophets of God and His chosen ones will seek its companionship. With them that soul will freely converse, and will recount unto them that which it hath been made to endure in the path of God, the Lord of all worlds. If any man be told that which hath been ordained for such a soul in the worlds of God, the Lord of the throne on high and of earth below, his whole being will instantly blaze out in his great longing to attain that most exalted, that sanctified and resplendent station . . . . "

Life, Death and Immortality, Compiled by Hayes, Fisher, Hill and Cassiday, Chapter Four, The Soul After Death, Baha'i Pubishing Trust, 1994, (Baha'i,

194
Words of Baha'u'llah)

Auspicious Words of the Successor to Baha'u'llah, his son Abdu'l-Baha

Abdul Baha   **Abdul Baha in Later Years**
(Bahai Distribution Service) AND ("Religions of the World" By Lewis M. Hopfe, From the Baha'i Distribution Service, Prentice Hall, 1994)

"You question about eternal life and the entrance into the Kingdom. The outer expression used for the Kingdom is heaven; but this is a comparison and similitude, not a reality or fact, for the Kingdom is not a material place; it is sanctified from time and place. It is a spiritual world, a divine world, and the center of the Sovereignty of God; it is freed from body and that which is corporeal, and it is purified and sanctified from the imaginations of the human world. To be limited to place is a property of bodies and not of spirits."

Some Answered Questions, No. 67, Page 241,
Translated by Laura Clifford Barney, Baha'i

Publishing Trust, 1930, (Baha'i)

CHAPTER TEN
Final Words According to the Prophet Baha'u'llah

"Wert thou to ponder in thine heart the behavior of the Prophets of God thou wouldst assuredly and readily testify that there must needs be other worlds besides this world. The majority of the truly wise and learned have, throughout the ages, as it hath been recorded by the Pen of Glory in the Tablet of Wisdom, borne witness to the truth of that which the holy Writ of God hath revealed. Even the materialists have testified in their writings to the wisdom of these divinely-appointed Messengers, and have regarded the references made by the Prophets to Paradise, to hell fire, to future reward and punishment, to have been actuated by a desire to educate and uplift the souls of men. Consider, therefore, how the generality of mankind, whatever their beliefs or theories, have recognized the excellence, and admitted the superiority, of these Prophets of God. These Gems of Detachment are acclaimed by some as the embodiments of wisdom, while others believe them to be the mouthpiece of God Himself. How could such Souls have consented to surrender themselves unto their enemies if they believed all the worlds of God to have been reduced to this earthly life? Would they have willingly suffered such afflictions and torments as no man hath ever experienced or witnessed?"

Life, Death and Immortality, Compiled by Hayes, Fisher, Hill and Cassiday, Chapter Four, The Worlds of God, Baha'i Pubishing Trust, 1994, (Baha'i, Words

198

of Baha'u'llah)

Near Death and Out-of-Body Experiences

(Auspicious Births and Deaths)

Of the Prophets, Saints, Mystics and Sages in World Religions

Out-of-Body Travel and Mysticism

Compiled by Marilynn Hughes

Photo by Harvey Kushner

Ever wanted to know about some of the most fascinating moments in religious history? Moments when prophets and world religions were born? Final words and moments of the great prophets? Out-of-Body Experiences which led to the prophet's missions? Near Death Experiences and Afterlife Visions experienced by the prophets, saints, mystics and sages?

If so, this book is for you! Culled from some of the most remote ancient texts on world religion, these expressive moments in religious history are compiled in the actual words of those who witnessed or recorded these events.

Go to our Website at:

www.outofbodytravel.org

For more information!

BIBLIOGRAPHY

Having made a shortened list of some of the more important texts of the world religions, I've made careful note to include texts which have been drawn to me in sacred vision and have been an integral part of energizing my spiritual path. Most of the texts in the bibliography have been brought to me through eternal guidance.

World Scripture is an excellent starting point, as it contains scripture from all world religions on various subjects, as well as, a detailed listing in back of the prescribed texts from all major and minor world religions.

Scriptural texts are the foundation or the root of knowledge. Visionary texts are the branches of the tree. Lives of prophets, saints, mystics and sages are the leaves.

Words in italics are actual book titles, while the unitalicized words are not title names, but rather authors and saints to glean from.

Hinduism: *The Bhagavad Gita As It Is, Srimad Bhagavatam, Upanishads, KRSNA, Autobiography of a Yogi, The Divine Romance, Man's Eternal Quest, The Gospel of Sri Ramakrishna*

Judaism: *New Jerusalem Bible, The Talmudic Anthology, The Zohar (Kaballah), The Apocrypha, The Lost Books of the Bible and the Forgotten Books of Eden, The Book of Enoch, Sefer haHinnuch, Josephus, Philo, The Way of God, The Path of the Just, The Gates of Repentance*

Zoroastrianism: *The Avesta, The Desatir, A Guide to Zoroastrian Religion*

Buddhism: *A Buddhist Bible, Dialogues of the Buddha, Dhammapada, Threefold Lotus Sutra, Path to Deliverance, The Flower Ornament Scripture, The Holy Teaching of Vimalakurti, Sutra of the Past Vows of Earth Store Bodhisattva, A Guide to the Bodhisattva's Way of Life, Training the Mind in the Great Way, The Life of the Buddha, Moon in a Dewdrop, The Shobogenzo, Tao Te Ching, Chuang Tsu, Analects of Confucius, Wen Tzu*

Christianity: *Holy Bible, Apocrypha, Lost Books of the Bible and the Forgotten Books of Eden, Dead Sea Scriptures, Gospel of Thomas, Essene Gospel of Peace 1-4, Book of Enoch, Nag Hammadi Library, Pistis Sophia, Gnosis on the Silk Road, The Dialogue of St. Catherine of Siena, The Mystical City of God, Heaven & Hell, The Life of Jesus Christ and Biblical Revelations, The Imitation of Christ*, and the writings of the saints with an emphasis on the following: St. Augustine, Mother Teresa, Padre Pio, St. Alphonsus Liguori, Cure' of Ars, St. Teresa of Avila, St. Thomas Aquinas, St. Francis de Sales, St. John Bosco, St. Ignatius, St. John of the Cross, Emanuel Swedenborg, Martin Luther, John Calvin

Islam: *Holy Qur'an, Sahih Muslim* (The Hadith), *Nahjul Balagha, Imam Gazzali's Ihya Ulum Ud Din, The Life of Mohammad (Translation of Sirat Rasul Allah), Signs of the Unseen, The Doctrine of the Sufi's*

Baha'i: *Tablets of Baha'u'llah, Seven Valleys and the Four Valleys, The Kitab-I-Iqan, The Hidden Words, Prayers and Meditations, Selections from the Writings of the Bab, Tablets of the Divine Plan, Promulgation of Universal Peace*

Mystery Religions: *The Divine Pymander of Hermes, The Emerald Tablets of Thoth, An Interpretation of the Emerald Tablets, The Ancient Mysteries, The Secret Doctrine of the Rosicrucians, Secret Teachings of All Ages, Plotinus: The Enneads,*

Tribal: *Book of the Hopi, Secrets of Mayan Science/Religion, Navajo Religion, Encyclopedia of Native American Religions, African Religions & Philosophy*

SOURCE LISTING

African Religions and Philosophy, by John S. Mbiti, Heinerman, 1969
Agony, of Jesus, The, by Padre Pio, Tan Books, 1967
Ahaveth Chesed, by the Chafetz Chaim, Feldheim Publishers, 1967
An Interpretation of the Emerald Tablets, by Doral, Brotherhood of the White Temple, 1992
An Introduction to the Devout Life, by St. Francis De Sales, Tan Books, 1923
Analects of Confucius, The, by Confucius, Translator Arthur Waley, Vintage Books, 1938
Ancient Mysteries, The, Editor Marvin W. Meyer, Harper Collins, 1987
Anguttara Nikaya 1-3, Translator Nyanaponika Thera, Buddhist Publication Society, 1981
Anugita, The, Translator Kashinath Trimbak Telang, Wizards Bookshelf, 1981
Apocrypha, The Editor Manuel Kromroff, Dorset Press, 1992
Apologia Pro Vita Sua, by John Henry Cardinal Newman, Doubleday Image Books, 1956
Aryasura's Aspiration/Meditation on Compassion, by Tenzin Gyatso, H.H. the 14th Dalai Lama, Library of Tibetan Works, 1975
Autobiography of a Yogi, by Paramahansa Yogananda, Self-Realization Fellowship, 1946
Autobiography of St. Margaret Mary, The, by Saint Margaret Mary, Tan Books, 1930
Avesta, The, Translator Rev. Ernestine Busch, Ernestine G. Busch, 1985
Baha'u'llah and the New Era, by J.E. Esslemont, Baha'i Publishing Trust, 1923
Being and Vibration, by Joseph Raphael and Mary Elizabeth Marlow, Council Oak Books, 1993
Bhagavad Gita, The, Translator Eknath Easwaran, Nilgri Press, 1985
Bhagavad-Gita As It Is, Translator A.C. Bhaktivedanta Swami, Bhaktivedanta Book Trust, 1986
Bible in Art, The, Editor Clifton Harby, Garden City Publishing Co., 1936
Birth of Purgatory, The, by Jacques Le Goff, Translator Arthur Goldhammer, The University of Chicago Press, 1981
Black Elk Speaks, by John G. Neihardt, University of Nebraska Press, 1932
Blessed Eucharist, The, by Fr. Michael Muller C.S.S.R., Tan Books, 1868
Book of Discipline, The, Translator I.B. Horner, Pali Text Society, 1938
Book of Analysis, The, Translator Pathamakyaw Ashin Thittila, Pali Text Society, 1969
Book of Enoch the Prophet, The, Translator Richard Laurence, Wizards Bookshelf, 1883
Book of the Hopi, by Frank Waters, Penguin Books, 1963
Buddhist Bible, A, Editor Dwight Goddard, Beacon Press, 1938
Call to Remembrance, by Baha'u'llah, Baha'i Publishing Trust, 1992
Candragomin's Twenty Verses on the Bodhisattva Vow, by Sakya Dragpa Gyaltsen, Library of Tibetan Works and Archives, 1982
Catechism of the Catholic Church, by The Holy See, Doubleday Image Books, 1994
Changeless Nature, The, by Arya Maitreya and Acarya Asanga, Translators Ken and Katia Holmes, Karma Drubgyud Darjay Ling, 1985

Chofetz Chaim Looks at: Eternity, The, by The Chofetz Chaim, Bais Yechiel Publications, 1989

Chuang Tsu, by Lao Tsu, Translators Gia-Fu Feng and Jane English, Random House, Vintage Books, 1974

City of God, by Saint Augustine, Translators Walsh, Zema, Monahan, Honan, Doubleday Image Books, 1950

Classic Midrah, The, Translator Reuven Hammer, Paulist Press, 1995

Collected Works of Saint John of the Cross, The, by Saint John of the Cross, Translators KieranVanaugh   and Otilio Rodriquez, ICS Publications, 1979

Complete Artscroll Siddur, The, Translator Rabbi Nosson Scherman, Mesorah Publications, Ltd., 1985

Complete Works of Josephus, The, by Flavius Josephus, Translator William Whiston A.M., Krege, 1960

Concise Book of Mitzvoth, The, Editor The Chafetz Chayim, The Feldheim Publishers, 1990

Confessions of Saint Augustine, The, by Saint Augustine, Translator Rex Warner, Penguin Books, Mentor, 1963

Contemplative Prayer, by Thomas Merton, Doubleday, 1969

Course in Miracles, The, by The Foundation for Inner Peace, Foundation for Inner Peace, 1975

Dead Sea Scriptures, The, Translator Theodore H. Gaster, Doubleday, Anchor Books, 1956

Denkoroku, The, by Keizan Zenji, Translator Rev. Hubert Nearman, Shasta Abbey Press, 1993

Desatir, The, Translator Mulla Firuz Bin Kaus, Wizards Bookshelf, 1888

Devotion for the Dying, by Mother Mary Potter, Tan Books, 1880

Dhammapada, Translator Harischandra Kaviratna, Theosophical University Press, 1980

Dialogue of Saint Catherine of Siena, Translator Algar Thorold, Tan Books, 1907

Dialogues of the Buddha, Translators T.W. and C.A.F. Rhys Davids and Scholars, Pali Text Society, 1921

Diamond Sutra and The Sutra of Hui-Neng, The, Translator A.F. Price and Wong Mou-lam, Shambhala   Publications, Inc. 1990

Discourse on the Fruits of Recluseship, The, Translator Bhikku Bodhi, Buddhist Publication Society, 1989

Divine Crucible of Purgatory, The, by Mother Mary of Saint Austin, Helper of Holy Souls, Unknown Publisher and Date

Divine Love and Wisdom, by Emanuel Swedenborg, Translator George F. Dole, Swedenborg Foundation, 1985

Divine Mercy In My Soul, by Sister M. Faustina, Translators Drabik, Pearce, Maguire, Marina Helpers, 1987

Divine Providence, by Emanuel Swedenborg, Swedenborg Foundation, 1764

Divine Pymander of Hermes, The, by Hermes Mercurius Trismegistus, Translator Dr. Everard, Wizards Bookshelf, 1978

Divine Romance, The, by Paramahansa Yogananda, Self-Realization Fellowship, 1986

Doctrine of the Sufi's, The, by Al-Kalabadhi, AMS Press, 1935

Druids, The, by Peter Berresford Ellis, William B. Eerfdmans Publishing Co.,

1994

Echoes in the Heavenly Court, Editor Dean of Machon, Feldheim Publishers, 1994

Edgar Cayce, Modern Prophet, by Carter, Hartzell, Reed, Langley, Gramercy Books, 1967

Egyptian Heaven and Hell, The, by E.A. Budge, Open Court, 1905

Emerald Tablets of the Thoth the Atlantean, The, by Thoth the Atlantean, Translator Doreal,   Brotherhood of the White Temple, 1939

Encyclopedia of Native American Religions, The, by Hirschfelder, Arlene and Molin, Paulette, MJF Books,   1992

Epistle to the Son of Wolf, by Baha'u'llah, Baha'i Publishing Trust, 1941

Essence of Self-Realization, The, by Kriyananda (J. Donald Walters), Crystal Clarity Publishers, 1990

Essene Book of Creation, The, by Edmond Bordeaux Szekely, International Biogenic Society, 1989

Essene Communications with the Infinite, by Edmond Bordeaux Szekely, International Biogenic Society, 1979

Essene Gospel of Peace, The, Vol. 1-4, Translator Edmond Bordeaux Szekely, International Biogenic Society, 1981

Essential Rumi, The, by Rumi, Translator Coleman Barks, HarperSanFrancisco, 1995

Ethics of Spinoza, The, by Baruch Spinoza, Carol Publishing Group, 1957

Fathers of the Church, The, Vol. 2, 4, 11, 16, 60, by Saint Augustine, Catholic University of America Press, 1947-1968

Five Books of Moses, The, Translator Everett Fox, Schocken, 1983

Flower Ornament Scripture, The, Translator Thomas Cleary, Shambhala Publications, 1984

Forgotten Secret of Fatima, The, by Msgr. Joseph A. Cirrincione and Thomas A. Nelson, Tan Books, 1988

Forty Dreams of Saint John Bosco, by Saint John Bosco, Tan, 1969

Four Doctrines, The, by Emanuel Swedenborg, Swedenborg Foundation, 1763

Fox's Book of Martyrs, by John Fox, Whitaker House, 1981

Gates of Repentance, The, by Rabbeinu Yonah Ben Avaham of Gerona, Feldheim Publishers, 1967

General Principles of Kabbalah, Rabbi Moses C. Luzzatto, Translator Dr. Philip S. Berg, Research Centre of Kabbalah, 1970

Ghost-Dance Religion and Wounded Knee, The, By James Mooney, Dover, (Original Publication) 1896, (Tribal: Ghost Dance Religion, Oglala Sioux)

Glories of Mary, The, by Saint Alphonsus Liguori, Redemptorist Fathers, 1931

Gnosis on the Silk Road, Translator Hans-Joachim Klimkeit, HarperSanFransisco, 1993

Gospel of Sri Ramakrishna, The, by M., a disciple of the holy Master, Translator Swami Nikhilananda, Ramakrishna-Vivekananda Center, 1942

Gospel of the Holy Twelve, The, Translator Rev. Gideon Jasper Richard Ousley, Teofil de la Torre, N.D., O.D., 1954

Gospel of Thomas, The, Translator Marvin Meyer, HarperSanFransisco, 1992

Grace Abounding, by John Bunyan, Whitaker House, 1993

Great Means of Salvation and of Perfection, The, by Saint Alphonsus Liguori, Redemptorist Fathers, 1927

Great Ocean-An Authorized Biography of the Dali Lama, by Roger Hicks and Ngakpa Chogyam, Penguin Books, 1984

Group of Discourses, The, Translator K.R. Norman, Pali Text Society, 1992

Guide to the Bodhisattva's Way of Life, A, by Shantideva, Translator Steven Batchelor, Library of Tibetan works and Archives, 1979

Guide to the Zoroastrian Religion, A, Translators Firoze M. Kotwal and James W. Boyd, Scholars Press, 1982

Heaven and Hell, by Emanuel Swedenborg, Translator George G. Dole, Swedenborg Foundation, 1976

Hell and How to Avoid Hell, by Fr. F.X. Schouppe S.J. and Thomas A. Nelson, Tan Books, 1989

Hidden Words and Selected Holy Writings, The, by Baha'u'llah, Baha'i Publishing Trust, 1985

Hildegard of Bingen's Book of Divine Works, Editor Matthew Fox, Bear & Co., 1987

History of Witchcraft, The, by Fr. Montague Summers, Barnes & Noble, 1993

Holy Bible, The (King James Version), World Bible Publishers, 1989

Holy Qur'an, by Muhammed, Translator Maulana Muhammed Ali, Ahmadiyyah Anjuman Isha'at Islam, 1917

Holy Teaching of Vimalakirti, The, Translator Robert A.F. Thurman, Pennsylvania State University, 1976

Hymns of Hermes, The, by G.R.S. Mead, Phanes Press, 1991

Hymns of the RGVEDA, Translator Ralph T.H. Griffith, Motilal Danarsidass, Date Unknown

Ihya 'Ulim-Ud-Din, by Imam Gazzali, Translator Al-Haj Maulana Fazal-Ul-Karim, Kazi Publications, Date Unknown

Imitation of Christ, The, by Thomas A. Kempis, Barbour & Co., 1984

Interior Castle, by Saint Teresa of Avila, Translator E. Allison Peers, Doubleday Dell, Image Books, 1961

Introduction to Saint Thomas Aquinas, Editor Anton C. Pegis, Random House, 1945

Itivuttaka, The, Translator John D. Ireland, Buddhist Publication Society, 1991

Jesus Christ 1 and 2, by Ferdinand Prat S.J., Translator John J. Heenan, S.J., Bruce Publishing Co., 1950

Kabbalah, by Gershom Scholem, Penguin Books, Meridian, 1974

Khutubat-I-Jumu'ah, Editor Maulana H. Ashraf Ali, Sh. Muhammad Ashraf, Date Unknown

KITAB-I-AQUDAS, The, by Baha'u'llah, Baha'i Publications, 1993

KITAB-I-IQAN, The, by Baha'u'llah, Baha'i Publishing Trust, 1931

KRSNA, Translator A.C. Bhaktivedanta Swami Prabhupada, Bhaktivedanta Book Trust, 1996

Kybalion, The, by Three Initiates, Yogi Publication Society, 1912

Large Sutra on Perfect Wisdom, The, Translator Edward Conze, University of California Press, 1975

Legends and Lore of the American Indians, Editor Terri Hardin, Barnes & Noble, 1993

Life and Glories of Saint Joseph, by Edward Healy Thompson M.A., Tan Books, 1888

Life and Holiness, by Thomas Merton, Doubleday, 1962

Life and Teaching of the Masters of the Far East, by Baird T. Spalding, DeVorss &Co., 1948

Life of Jesus Christ and Biblical Revelations, The, by Ven. Anne Catherine Emmerich, Tan Books, 1914

Life of Muhammad, The, Editor A. Guillaume, Oxford University Press, 1995

Life of the Blessed Virgin Mary, The, by Ven. Anne Catherine Emmerich, Translator Sir Michael Palairet, Tan Books, 1954

Life of the Buddha, The, Translator Bhikku Nanamoli, Buddhist Publication Society, 1972

Little Flowers of Saint Francis, The, by Brother Ugolino di Monte Santa Maria, Translator Raphael Brown, Doubleday Image, 1958

Living Buddha, Living Christ, by Thich Naht Hahn, Parallax Press, 1995

Lost Books of the Bible/Forgotten Books of Eden, Translator World Bible Publishers/Alpha House, World Bible Publishers, 1926

Love of Christ, The, by Mother Teresa, Translator John A. Otto, Harper & Row, 1982

Maggid of Dubno and his Parables, The, by Benno Heinemann, Feldheim Publishers, 1967

Mahabharata, The, Editor C. Narasimhan, Columbia University Press, 1965

Man and God, by Voctor Gollancz, Houghton Mifflin, 1950

Man's Eternal Quest, by Paramahansa Yogananda, Self-Realization Fellowship, 1975

Mansions of the Soul, by H. Spencer Lewis, Supreme Grand Lodge of AMORC, 1930

Marital Love, by Emanuel Swedenborg, Swedenborg Foundation, 1768

Masters of the Path, by Dr. Javad Nurbakhsh, Khaniqanhi-Nimatullahi Publications, 1980

Meaning of Life, The, by Tenzin Gyasto H.H. the 14th Dalai Lama, Wisdom Publications, 1992

Mediaeval Legends of Christ, by A.S. Rapport Ph.D., Nicholson, Ivor, & Watson, 1934

Meditation Prayer on Mary Immaculate, by Padre Pio, Translator Laura Chanler White, Tan Books, 1974

Moments Divine Before the Blessed Sacrament, by Fr. Frederick A. Reuter K.C.B.S., Tan Books, 1922

Moon in a Dewdrop, Editor Kazuaki Tanahashi, North Point Press, 1985

My Utmost for His Highest, by Oswald Chambers, Barbour and Co., 1935

Mystical City of God, by Ven. Mary of Agreda, Translator Fiscar Marison, Blue Army of Our Lady of Fatima, 1949

Mystical City of God, The, Abridged, by Ven. Mary of Agreda, Tan Books, 1978

Mystical Life of Jesus, The, by H. Spencer Lewis, Supreme Grand Lodge of AMORC, 1929

Mystical Visions, by Hildegard Von Bingen, Bear & Co., 1986

Nag Hammadi Library, The, Translator Coptic Gnostic Library Project, Harper Collins, 1978

Nahjul Balagha, by Imam Ali Ibn Abu Talib, Translator Sayed Ali Reza, Tahrike Tarsile Qur'an, Unknown

Native Religions of North America, by Ake Hultkrantz, HarperSanFransisco, 1987

Navajo Religion, by Gladys A. Reichard, Princeton University Press, 1950

Nectar of Devotion, The, by A.C. Bhaktivedanta Swami Prabhupada, Bhaktivedanta Book Trust, 1970

Nectar of Instruction, The, Translator A.C. Bhaktivedanta Swami Prabhupada, Bhaktivedanta Book Trust, 1975

New American Bible, The, World Bible Publishers, 1970

New Jerusalem Bible, The, Doubleday, 1985

New Oxford Annotated Bible, The, Oxford University Press, 1946

On Christian Doctrine, by Saint Augustine, Translator D.W. Robertson Jr., Macmillan, 1958

On Evil, by Saint Thomas Aquinas, Translator Jean Oesterle, University of Notre Dame Press, 1995

On Free Choice of Will, by Saint Augustine, Translators Anna Benjamin and L.H. Hackstaff, Library of Liberal Arts, 1964

On the Kabbalah and its Symbolism, by Gershom Scholem, Translator Ralph Manheim, Schocken Books, 1965

Orations of Muhammad, The, by M. Muhammad Abaidul Akbar, Sh. Muhammad Ashraf, 1954

Our Lady of Fatima's Peace Plan From Heaven, Tan Books, 1950

Padre Pio: The True Story, by C. Bernard Ruffin, Our Sunday Visitor, 1982

Path of Discrimination, The, Translator Bhikku Nanamoli, Pali Text Society, 1991

Path of Purification, The, by Bhadantacariya Buddhagosa, Translator Bhikku Nanamoli, Buddhist Publication Society, 1975

Path of the Just, The, by Rabbi Moshe Chaim Luzzatto, Feldheim Publishers, 1966

Path of the Righteous Gentile, The, by Chaim Clorfene and Yakov Rogalsky, Feldheim Publishers, 1987

Path of Yoga, The, by A.C. Bhaktivedanta Swami Parbhupada, Bhaktivedanta Book Trust, 1971, 1979

Path to Deliverance, by Nyanatiloka Mahathera, Buddhist Publication Society, 1952

Path to Enlightenment, The, by Tenzin Gyatso, H.H. the 14th Dalai Lama, Snow Lion Publications, 1995

Philosophies and Religions of India, The, by Yogi Ramacharaka, Yogi Publication Society, 1930

Pilgrim's Progress, The, by John Bunyan, Barbor & Co., 1993

Pistis Sophia, Translator G.R.S. Mead, Kessinger Publishing Co., Date Unknown

Plotinus: The Enneads, by Plotinus, Translator Stephen MacKenna, Larson Publications, 1992

Prayers and Heavenly Promises, by Joan Carroll Cruz, Tan Books, 1990

Prayers and Meditations, by Baha'u'llah, Translator Shoghi Effendi, Baha'i Publishing Trust, 1938

Prayers of Saint Francis, The, Editor W. Bader, New City Press, 1988

Prayertimes with Mother Teresa, by Eileen and Kathleen Egan, Doubleday, 1989

Preparation for Death, by Saint Alphonsus Liguori, Translator Robert A. Coffin, Tan Books, 1857

Promulgation of Universal Peace, The, by Abdul-Baha, Baha'i Publishing Trust, 1982

Prophet, The, by Kahlil Gibran, Walker & Co., 1923

Purgatory, by Fr. F.X. Schouppe S.J., Tan Books, 1926

Pyramidology (Three Volumes), by Adam Rutherford, Institute of Pyramidology, 1957

Pythagorean Sourcebook and Library, The, Translators Guthrie, Taylor, Fairbanks, Phanes Press, 1987

Rama Story, The, by Bhagavan Sri Sathya Sai Baba, Translator N. Kasturi, Sri Sathya Sai Books and Publications, 1981

Red Record, The, Translator David McCutchen, Pavery Publishing Group, Inc., 1993

Reincarnation, An East-West Anthology, Editors Head and Cranston, Theosophical Publishing House, 1961

Revelations of Divine Love, by Juliana of Norwich, Translator M.L. del Mastro, Image Doubleday, 1977

Revelations of Saint Bridget, by Saint Bridget, Tan Books, 1965

Rosary Novenas to Our Lady, by Charles V. Lacey, Benziger, 1926

Sacred Pipe, The, by Joseph Epes Brown, Norman & London, University of Oklahoma Press, 1953

Saddharma-Pundarika or the Lotus of the True Law, Translator H. Kern, Dover Publications, 1963

Sahih Muslim (The Hadith, Volumes 1-4), by Imam Muslim, Translator Abdul Hamid Siddiqi, Nusrat Ali Nasri for Kitab Bhavan, Date Unknown

Samyutta Nikaya 1-3, Translator John D. Ireland, Buddhist Publication Society, 1981

Sayings of Paramahansa Yogananda, by Paramahansa Yogananda, Self-Realization Fellowship, 1952

Science of Being and Art of Living, The, by Mahrishi Manhesh Yogi, International SRM Publications, 1966

Secret Doctrine of the Rosicrucians, The, by Magus Incognito, Yoga Publication Society, 1949

Secret Doctrines of Jesus, The, by H. Spencer Lewis, AMORC, 1937

Secret of Divine Civilization, The, by Abdul-Baha, Baha'i Publishing Trust, 1957

Secret of the Rosary, The, by Saint Louis Mary De Montfort, Translator Mary Barbour, Montfort Publications, 1965

Secret Teachings of All Ages, The, by Manly P. Hall, Philosophical Research Society, 1977

Secrets of Mayan Science/Religion, by Hunbatz Men, Translators Diana Ayala and James II Dunlap, Bear & Co., 1990

Sefer haHinnuch, Ascribed to: Rabbi Aaron of Barcelona haLevi, Feldheim Publishers, 1523

Selections from the Writings of the BA'B, by The BA'B, Translator Habib Taherzadeh, Baha'i World Centre, 1976

Sepher Yezirah, Translator Dr. Isidor Kalish, L.H. Frank & Co., 1877

Sermon on the Mount According to Vedanta, The, by Swami Prabhavananda, New American Library, 1963

Seven Valleys and the Four Valleys, The, by Baha'u'llah, Baha'i Publishing Trust, 1945

Shobogenzo-Zuimonki, Translator Shohaku Okumura, Kyoto Soto-Zen Center, Date Unknown

Sign of Contradiction, by Karol Wojytla (Pope John Paul II), Seabury Press, 1979
Signs of the Unseen, by Rumi, Translator W.M. Thackston Jr., Threshold Books, 1994
Sinner's Guide, The. by Ven. Louis of Granada, O.P., Tan Books, 1883
Some Answered Questions, by Abdul-Baha', Baha'i Publishing Trust, 1930
Son of the Sun, by Savitri Devi, Supreme Grand Lodge of A.M.O.R.C., 1946
Songs of the Soul, by Paramahansa Yogananda, Self-Realization Fellowship, 1983
Soul Sanctified, The, Tan Books, 1873
Speaking in Tongues, by Felicitias D. Goodman, University of Chicago Press, 1972
Spiritual Combat, The, by Dom Lorenzo Scupoli, Translators William Lester and Robert Mohan, Tan Books, 1945
Spiritual Doctrine of Saint Catherine of Genoa, The, by Saint Catherine of Genoa, Tan Books, 1874
Spiritual Exercises of Saint Ignatius, The, by Saint Ignatius, Translator Anthony Mottola Ph.d, Image Books, 1964
Sri Guru Granth Sahib, (4 Volumes), Translator Gurbachan Singh Talib, Publication Bureau, Punjabi   University, 1995
Srimad Bhagavatam (Volumes 1-3), Translator A.C. Bhaktivedanta Swami Prabhupada, Bhaktivedanta Book Trust, 1972
Srimad Bhagavatam (Part One), Translator A.C. Bhadtivedanta Swami Prabhupada, Bhaktivedanta Book Trust 1975
Srimad Bhagavatam (An Abridgement), Translator Swami Prabhavananda, Sri Ramakrishna Math, Date Unknown
Saint Antony of the Dessert, by Saint Athanasius, Translator Dom J.B. McLaughlin, Tan Books, 1924
Saint Athanasius On the Incarnation, by Saint Athanasuis, Translators Religious of C.S.M.V.A., Saint Vladimirs, 1944
Saint Francis of Assisi, by Saint Francis of Assisi, Thomas Nelson Publishers, 1989
Saint Michael and the Angels, Compiled from approved sources, Tan Books, 1977
Story of A Soul, by Saint Therese of Lisieux, Translator John Clark .C.D., ICS, 1975
Strive for Truth, Volumes 1-3, by Rabbi Eliyahu E. Dessler, Feldheim Publishers, 1978
Sutra of the Past Vows of Earth Store Bodhisattva, Translator Heng Ching, Buddhist Text Translation Society,   1974
Tablets of Baha'u'llah, by Baha'u'llah, Translator Habib Taherzadeh, Baha'i Publishing Trust, 1978
Tablets of the Divine Plan, by Abdul-Baha', Baha'i Publishing Trust, 1977
Taharas Halashon, Translator David Landesman, Feldheim Publishers, 1994
Talmud, The, Classics of Western Spirituality Series, Paulist Press, 1989
Talmudic Anthology, The, Editor Spitz Newman, Behrman House, Inc., 1945
Tao Te Ching, by Lao Tsu, Translators Gia-Fu Feng and Jane English, Random House, Vintage Books, 1972
Tao Te Ching, by Lao Tsu, Translator Victor H. Mair (from the Ma-Wang-Tui Manuscripts), Bantam, 1990

Teachings of Lord Caitanya, Translator A.C. Bhativedanta Swami Parabhupada, Bhakivedanta Book Trust, 1985
Teachings of Lord Kapila, Translator A.C. Bhativedanta Swami Parabhupada, Bhakivedanta Book Trust, 1977
Teachings of Queen Kunti, by A.C. Bhativedanta Swami Parabhupada, Bhativedanta Book Trust, 1978
Teachings of Sri Ramakrishna, by Advaita Ashrama, Swami Mumukshananda, 1994
Teachings of Sri Sarada Devi ,the Holy Mother, Editor Sri Ramakrishna Math, Sri Ramakrishna Math, Date Unknown
Teachings of Swami Vivekananda, Editor Advaita Ashrama, Advaita Ashrama, 1994
Theology of Saint Paul, The, by Fernand Prat S.J., The Newman Bookshop, 1926
Therese Neumann, by Adalbert Albert Vogl, Tan Books, 1987
Third Secret of Fatima, The, by Brother Michael of the Holy Trinity, Translator Anne Barbeau Gardiner, Tan Books, 1991
Thoughts and Sayings of Saint Margaret Mary, by Saint Margaret Mary, Tan Books, 1935
Three Pure Land Sutras, The, by Hisao Inagaki, by Nagata Bunshodo, 1994
Three Ways of the Spiritual Life, The, by Rev. R. Garrigou-Lagrange O.P., Tan Books, 1938
Threefold Lotus Sutra, The, Translators Kato, Tamura, Miyasaka, Kosei Publishing Co., 1971
Tibetan Book of the Dead, The, Editor W.Y. Evans-Wentz, Oxford University Press, 1960
Tibetan Book of the Great Liberation, The, Editor W.Y. Evans-Wentz, Oxford University Press, 1954
Torah, The, Translator Jewish Publication Society of America, Jewish Publication Society of America, 1962
Training the Mind in the Great Way, by Gyalwa Gendun Druppa (The First Dalai Lama), Translator Glenn H.   Mullin, Snow Lion Publications, 1993
Travelers Narrative, A, by Abdul-Baha', Translator Edward G.Browne, Baha'i Publishing Trust, 1980
Treasury of Judaism, A, Editor Philip Birnbaum, Hebrew Publishing, 1957
Trinity, The, by Saint Augustine, Translator Edmund Hill O.P., New City Press, 1991
True Christian Religion, The, by Emanuel Swedenborg, Swedenborg Foundation, 1771
True Devotion to Mary, by Saint Louis De Montfort, Translator Fr. Federick Faber, Tan Books, 1941
Twleve Steps to Holiness and Salvation, The, by Saint Alphonsus Liguori, Translators Rev. Paul Leik and Rev. Cornelius Warren, Tan Books, 1986
Udana, The, Translator John D. Ireland, Buddhist Publication Society, 1990
Unknown Life of Jesus Christ, The, by Nicolas Notovitch, Translator Alexina Loranger, Tree of Life Publications, 1894
Upanishands, The, Translator Eknath Easwaran, Nilgiri Press, 1987
Urantia Book, The, by Urantia, Urantia Foundation, 1955
Vedanta-Sutras, by Vyasadeva, Translator George Thibaut, Motial Banarsidass Publishers, 1904

Voice of the Saints, The, Editor Francis Johnston, Tan Books, 1965

Walking in the Sacred Manner, by Mark St. Pierre and Tilda Long Soldier, Simon & Schuster, 1995

Way of Divine Love, The, by Sister Josefa Menendez, Tan Books, 1972

Way of Perfection, The, by Saint Teresa of Avila, Translator E. Allison Peers, Doubleday Dell, Image Books, 1964

Way of the Sufi, The, by Idries Shah, Arkana Penguin Books, 1968

Ways of Reason, The, by Rabbi Moshe Chaim Luzzatto, Feldheim Publishers, 1989

Wen-Tzu, by Lao-tzu, Translator Thomas Cleary, Shambhala Publications, 1991

Whispers From Eternity, Paramahansa Yogananda, Self-Realization Fellowship, 1949

Wisdom of the Elders, by David Suzuki and Peter Knudtson, Bantam Books, 1992

Wisdom of the Idiots, by Idries Shah, Octagon Press, 1969

Wonders of the Holy Name, The, by Fr. Paul O'Sullivan O.P. (E.D.M.), Tan Books, 1946

Word of the Buddha, The, Translator Nyanatiloka, Buddhist Publication Society, Date Unknown

Works of Philo, The, by Philo, Translator C.D. Yonge, Hendrickson, 1995

World Scripture, by the International Religious Foundation, International Religious Foundation, 1991

Zohar, The, Translators Harry Sperling and Maurice Simon, Soncio Press Ltd., 1984

Look for these texts by going to:
www.bookfinder.com
or
www.sacred-texts.com!

Go to our Website at:
www.outofbodytravel.org
For more information!

LaVergne, TN USA
28 March 2011
221895LV00007B/50/A